Frome Society for L[

Marston Mill in 1975

Cooper & Tanner Sale Brochure

Relatives of Clara Grant with members of FSLS and guests at the unveiling of the plaque on 13th November 2015   *Photo: Judith Macarthur*

FOREWORD

It has been an exciting opportunity for me to chair the Frome Society for Local Study in my first year and to meet the dedicated team of volunteers who organise this extraordinary organisation. With nearly 450 members of the Society, the enthusiastic committee meet monthly to monitor and complete the many tasks required. Sub-committees efficiently organise the winter lecture season and the summer visits to places of interest. Significant additional tasks are the production of our magazine CONTACT and the annual completion of this, our annual Year Book.

We are indebted to the authors of these excellent articles and to Alastair MacLeay for his skilled editing. Janet and Cliff Howard have worked extremely hard to take on the production side so swiftly after the sad death of Alan Yeates earlier in the year.

The book contains a superb collection of articles that relate to Frome and the surrounding area. A number are extensively illustrated with images and maps that bring to life many of the stories being told. In particular the "Curious history of Marston Mill" by Robert Heath has a significant number of pictures that provide the evidence for his conclusions.

John Jolliffe describes the beliefs and bravery of bishops in the 17th century. We read of Bishop Ken, after defying the infamous George Jeffreys the "hanging judge", firmly refusing accommodation to the King's favourite, Nell Gwyn, eventually becoming the Bishop of Bath and Wells and spending his final years at Longleat.

After his talk to the Society last season, Keith Falconer extends our knowledge of Brunswick Place and the occupancy by the Rossetti family, Hilary Daniel has provided us with a most interesting account of Warfare in the West Country, and there is a further instalment of the diary of John Allen Giles. Margery Hyde writes of Jane Sinkins née Hine, "a force to be reckoned with", and an excerpt from the autobiography of Clara Grant, the extraordinary headmistress whose plaque was erected in Frome in November 2015, is included.

Peter Clark contributes a report of Gladstone's visit to Frome, as dramatised in the 2014 Frome Festival, and we are brought closer to the present day by David Millard's item on Frome Market and Diana Crossman's remembrances of St John's Ambulance Brigade. Reference to Rev WJE Bennett's problems with the smoke from the Silk Mill and correspondence concerning fox hunting complete the volume, which ends with an obituary to Alan Yeates by the editor.

Julian Watson

Chairman

CONTENTS

Exhuming Oldfield
An investigation into the curious history of Marston Mill, Spring Gardens
by Robert Heath

Background

Marston Mill lies in a valley about a mile north of Frome, at the end of a long elevated driveway off Jeffries Lane. The area is known nowadays as Spring Gardens, and is situated north of Bradford Bridge, east of Murtry Bridge, south of Orchardleigh, and west of Oldford. The Mells Brook flows east to west through the valley, later joining the Frome River and proceeding onwards to the Avon at Freshford.

Spring Gardens is a tranquil area beloved by dog-walkers, and many will know our mill from walking the footpaths which cross the fields in front of it. When you look around nowadays it is hard to imagine that 200 years ago this was an industrial landscape, with six mills spread over a distance of less than ¾ mile, the largest a massive six storey cloth factory. This and two others have since been dismantled stone by stone, one is converted to flats, and another is a house. The sole survivor, Marston Mill, was grinding and mixing grain as recently as 1976, operated by the Ellis family.

When we acquired the property in 2010 its past history was confusing. The estate agent's particulars claimed there had been a mill on the site since Roman times, that the current mill buildings dated back to 1460 when the previous mill was destroyed by a fire, and that it had been owned by the Champneys Family of Orchardleigh as early as 1543. However, the listed buildings entry stated it to be a 16th century building, rebuilt in the 19th century, and an auction brochure from 1975 describes the mill as having been built in the early 17th century. Despite these disparities there seemed to be a consensus that the property was a flourmill with an attached house for the miller and his family, both of which had been substantially rebuilt in Georgian or Victorian times.

Description of the Property

The main residential part of the property, Marston Mill House (*Fig 1*), is 115' long in total, 70' of which is of three storeys, constructed of rubble stone under a stone tile roof, and the remaining 45' is a single storey ex-stable building of rubble stone under a clay tiled roof. Excavations of the foundations of the house during the construction of the soakaway show it is built on a bed of packed clay and limestone boulders, about 100 yards south of the course of the Mells Brook. A major rebuilding programme took place in 1996 and no original external joinery remains, but there is still an old stone Georgian canopy over what was once the front door to the miller's house.

Attached to the western end of the house, forming an 'L', is a large four storey mill building measuring roughly 50' x 25' (*Fig 2*). This mill is oriented north-south across a channel which leaves the Mells Brook at a weir about 450 yards west of the property. The channel passes through the mill building and the mill race re-joins the Mells about 170 yards to the east.

Fig 1 Marston Mill House from the south

Fig 2 Marston Mill House and Mill from the north

The interior of the mill appears to have been constructed no earlier than the 19th century. The three upper floors are of machine cut 7"x1½" softwood planks with 1" steel tongues instated between each plank to prevent dust and debris falling through the gaps. The power comes from a vertical Francis turbine manufactured and installed by Gilkes in 1899, still in situ. This originally drove three 48" millstones two of which are also in situ. The building itself is of rubble stone construction with some rough ashlar quoins to the corners, and has a roof of triple Roman tiles with a pitch of about 48°.

There are signs that the mill building was originally about half the length, and the shape of the turbine flume suggests it once housed an external 6' wide 14' diameter breast-shot water wheel attached to the northern gable. It also appears that the height of the building was raised by around 4' to allow the insertion of a full-length grain storage floor. There are three massive buttresses on the western wall, and two on the eastern wall, we assumed because the vibration caused by the three millstones operating together was in danger of shaking the building to pieces.

Initial Investigation

The auction brochure shows the grain milling operation occupying not just the mill building but the whole of the house west of the main central chimney stack, leaving a relatively modest miller's house of only 35' x 20' to the east. Originally divided into two rooms downstairs, this space is now occupied by a single large sitting room measuring 30' by 15'. This has three oak ceiling beams with 4" wide chamfers (*Fig 3*) and an especially impressive inglenook fireplace, comprising two piers of massive stones spanned by an 11' bressumer beam with cross-section of 22" x 13" (*Fig 4*). The bressumer shows signs of a 4'6" wide fireplace having been inserted into it at some later stage, and both it and the ceiling beams have been distressed so they could be plastered over.

Fig 3 Chamfered sitting room ceiling beams   *Fig 4 Sitting room fireplace with bressumer beam*

Wide chamfers are a characteristic of medieval beams, and this suggested to us that the beams and the fireplace were likely to be part of the original building which had been refurbished and improved. In 2014 we commissioned a dendrochronological survey of the house to try to establish the age of this original building. The results dated the roof timbers in the main part of the house to 1746-7, confirming that the roof was replaced in the reign of George II, a little earlier than the listed buildings entry indicated. Sadly the ceiling beams in the sitting room could not be dated, as they were fast-growing oak, and had too few rings. This is apparently quite common, as fast growing oak is a great deal stronger and more flexible than slow growing oak, and is therefore much better for beams which need to take regular stress. However, what was something of a surprise was the date of the bressumer beam over the fireplace; this beam was apparently felled sometime between 1506 and 1507, at the end of the reign of Henry VII.

One theory was that this bressumer might have been brought into the house at a later date. However, the size of the pier stones and the surface distressing suggests that it, and indeed the beams, are most probably original and in situ. There are also some other features which suggest that the house might be older than generally thought. For example, there are some massive flagstones on the floor of the main sitting room which were apparently found 8" below the level of the current floor, one of which measuring 4' x 5' reportedly had burn marks on the reverse.

A breakthrough occurred when Robin Thornes, who in the past has audited ancient buildings for English Heritage, identified what we had thought was a buttress on the eastern wall of the mill as a disused external chimney breast attached to the northern wall of the house (*Fig 5*). He also discovered inside this wall the outline of a large fireplace which had at some stage been removed (*Fig 6*).This meant that the western half of the house was residential in the past, not part of the mill, so it seemed that rather than a 35' miller's cottage, we might have a 70' long house dating back over 500 years.

Fig 5 Chimney stack on north wall, shown by dotted line, in corner between the house and the mill building, with a window inserted in it.

Fig 6 Older flue outline visible behind an inserted brick fireplace which itself contains a newer stone fireplace.

A house of this size, with not just one but two fireplaces, is certainly not the sort of modest home you would expect a miller and his family to have lived in, so with the assistance of various local experts, including Michael McGarvie, we set about the task of trying to find out what we could about the history of the house.

The first thing we discovered was that Marston Mill was originally not part of Orchardleigh, but was sited in a detached portion of the Manor of Marston Bigot: hence the name Marston Mill. This parish was only transferred to Frome in 1885[1] and the name Spring Gardens is thought to have been coined by George Sheppard as recently as 1776.[2] Part of the area in 1791 was also referred to as the hamlet of Bradford Bridge[3], after the medieval bridge over the river Frome. However, a map showing Frome prior to 1750 clearly labels the specific area of Marston Mill, lying south of Brookover Farm and the Mells Brook, as Oldfield (*Fig 7*).

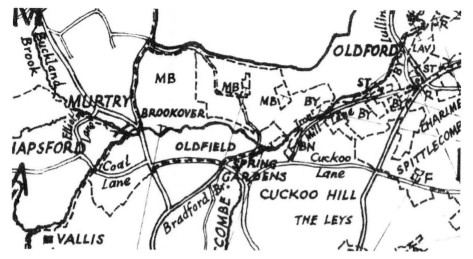

Fig 7 Map showing Oldfield prior to 1750, J H Harvey 1979

The History of Marston Mill

Mills have always been important buildings, and were usually as well documented as manor houses. Both Marston Bigot and Orchardleigh are shown in Domesday as having mills, but Marston Mill is not recorded in the Somerset Online Archive. The Marston Mill in Domesday would most likely have been south of Frome in the main Marston Bigot Estate, and as Marston Mill was part of the Manor of Marston Bigot, it isn't likely to have been the mill referred to in the Orchardleigh Domesday entry. But it did make us wonder how old Marston Mill really was, and what it was used for in the past?

Marston Mill had on its land a set of five sluices (Five Hatches) which used to be closed to irrigate the fields further down the valley. The agreement over the opening and closing of the hatches shows that in 1863 our mill was called Marston Mill, but digging further back we found Spring Gardens was very heavily populated with mills in the 19th century. At least four are identifiable on Greenwood's map of 1822, in order east to west:

1 White Mill. This lies in Orchardleigh.
2 A mill on the site of Sheppard's Mill. Sheppard's Mill was a huge six storey woollen mill built by George Sheppard from 1809 onwards. It ceased working after a fire in 1883 and was demolished in the 1960s.[4]
3 A mill on the site of Jeffries Mill, close to and north-west of Sheppard's Mill. This building was also a woollen mill, probably built in the early 19th century, and is now split into residential flats.[5]
4 A further mill on the site of Marston Mill

A map by Day, drawn up in 1782 shows the main drive to Orchardleigh passing along present-day Jeffries Lane and up the hill where a footpath now runs. Marston Mill and Jeffries Mill were situated to the west of this road, all in Marston Bigot, and this is

9

confirmed by the tithe map of the Marston Bigot Parish, which also shows a clear 'L' shaped building at the location of Marston Mill, confirming that the present mill building and house were in place in 1839. Sheppard's Mill was shown as being in Frome Parish. Of the four mills only White Mill lies in Orchardleigh, which makes it the most likely candidate for the Orchardleigh Domesday mill.

There were at least two other mills in this vicinity: Murtry apparently had a mill dating back to Domesday, but this was located in Buckland Dinham Parish. A further mill known as Kirty's Mill (now known simply as Iron Mill) was an edge-tool workshop, and this was situated downstream of White Mill and also outside Marston Bigot. But it seems there was another edge tool mill in this area: Robin Thornes writes in 'Men of Iron':

Kirty's Mill does not seem to have been the only edge tool works in the vicinity, the Orchardleigh map of 1816 showing a second building, labelled Iron Mill, to the west of Kirty's in a small detached portion of Marston Bigot. Little is known about this works, although it may have been occupied by Charles Hooper, an edge tool maker of Marston Bigot who was declared bankrupt in 1824.... In 1828 Charles, who was still living at Spring Gardens, Marston Bigot, patented an 'improved machine for shearing and cropping woollen and other cloths".[6]

Marston Mill is certainly upstream of Kirty's mill, and since we knew that Jeffries and Sheppard's mills were woollen mills, Marston Mill might have been Hooper's edge tool works. In order to explore this hypothesis, we turned to the writings of Ken Rogers. Using local land tax assessment records, he identifies 15 mill residents, tenants, and owners in Spring Gardens during the early 19th century.[7] Both the Fussells (edge tool manufacturers) and the Champneys family of Orchardleigh seem to have been owners of mills in Spring Gardens, as were the Jeffries family and William Sheppard. There is also a reference to a Thomas Collins, who was a 'cloth and wool dyer of Marston' in 1808, which means it was possible that Marston Mill was a fulling mill, used to bulk out woollen cloth. However there is no mention of Hooper.

So there were a number of candidates for the operators of Marston Mill, and a number of possible uses (flourmill, fulling mill, edge tool mill, cloth or wool factory, etc).

Then a completely new thought emerged, prompted by the curious leat arrangement of Marston Mill. A leat is a level channel used to take water from the main channel of a river to the mill. The water, by now higher than the river, passes through the mill, and the mill race takes it back at a lower level to the main river. Most old mills are sited on weirs, and have a very short leat or sometimes no leat at all, but the Marston Mill leat, shown in red on a copy of the Ordnance Survey Map of 1886 (*Fig 8*), is very long indeed, over 450 metres. Aside from the gentle curve at the start and a deviation around a rocky outcrop, it is also very straight; it was clearly purpose-built at great expense.

Fig 8 Extract from Somerset Ordnance Survey Map of 1886, Marston Mill leat shown in red.

One reason for this leat is the siting of Marston Mill. The OS map shows that the main channel of the Mells Brook in Spring Gardens winds in quite evident meanders across what is a flat area at the bottom of the valley. Sheppard's Mill, Jeffries Mill, White Mill, and even Kirty's Mill were all sited on or very close by the winding river, and operated off weirs or relatively short leats. Marston Mill, in contrast, is situated over 100 yards from the Mells Brook, which is why it needed such a long leat.

Why place a mill at such a distance away from the river, why not build it closer? Something we thought might explain this anomaly is the proximity of the Marston Mill leat to the old Dorset & Somerset Canal channel. The Dorset & Somerset Canal was never completed, but major earthworks were commenced between 1790 and 1800, and a section of these earthworks runs in parallel to the curved half of the Marston Mill leat. So it seemed possible that the leat might have been dug while the canal construction was taking place, with the spoil being used to raise the very high canal embankment. If this is the case, then the present Marston Mill site may only have become a mill at the end of the 18th century, when interest in cloth and edge-tool milling was at its peak.

To investigate this, we consulted Derrick Hunt, an expert on the Dorset and Somerset Canal, who produced the map surveyed by Bennett in 1795 to support the 1796 Act of Parliament giving assent to the building of the canal.[8] On it the Marston Mill area (*Fig 9*) can be seen clearly, but the leat is already there… and Marston Mill is labelled Mr Cooke's Mill, so the idea that the mill was built and the leat dug in 1800 was clearly wrong.

Fig 9 Dorset & Somerset Canal Survey Map, W Bennett 1795

11

The map also gave us a completely new mill with another new name: Trehearne Mill. Trehearne Mill is not shown on the 1822 map, and is situated at the point downstream of Jeffries Mill where the Frome and the Mells Brook run parallel to one another. Neither Trehearne nor Cooke appear as names of millers in Ken Rogers' list, so the operators of mills and the names of those mills changed very frequently!

As we seemed to be having little luck trying to work backwards, we decided to approach the search from the other end of the timeline, and investigate why this 'detached portion of Marston Bigot' to the north of Frome was retained by the Marston Bigot estate.

The Marston Bigot Estate

The land surrounding Marston Mill known as Oldfield is completely separate from Marston Bigot and nearly three miles away from the main estate. It is also a very small area compared with the large lands held to the south of Frome: The Marston Bigot Estate Map of 1839 shows a total holding of 2,238 acres, and this detached northern portion was only about 100 acres.

Michael McGarvie writes that the Spring Gardens portion was retained because '...the river Frome flowed through it and there were valuable Mills on its banks'.[9] This was undoubtedly true in the late 18th and early 19th century, when Marston / Cooke's Mill, Jeffries Mill, and Trehearne Mill, would all have lain within this portion of Marston Bigot, but if all of these mills were relatively recent, that would not explain the value this small portion of land had in historical times.

A clue however came from the history of the family who added the strange name of Bigot to Marston. The Bigots were a highly influential family, headed by the Earl of Norfolk, Marshal of England, and, as McGarvie says, "... a thorn in the side of English monarchs from the time of Henry II to the reign of Edward I".[10] It is likely they were given the manor of Marston sometime in the late 12th century either for services rendered or to prevent them causing trouble, and the earliest occupant seems to have been a Richard le Bigod. The first written reference to the family is in 1195, when Robert le Bigot is recorded as possessing the Manor of Marston. Robert passed the manor to his son Hugh, who in turn passed it to his son Robert 2. However, Robert 2 died childless, and the estate passed to his brother, Richard 2. And here 'The Book of Marston Bigot' contains a very interesting passage:

> 'Richard (2) is described as of 'Aldfeld', (Oldfield) in a charter dated between 1225 and 1233, in which he gave some land and a mill there to Cirencester Abbey... Richard lived in Spring Gardens, anciently called Oldfield, perhaps before succeeding to the main estate. The Mill was held by Alice, daughter of Peter Panel'.[11]

It therefore looked very likely that this might have been how this detached portion of land at Spring Gardens became part of the Marston Bigot estate. Richard 2, as the younger brother of Robert 2, seems to have had his own land and mill at Oldfield, and when he came into the Marston Bigot estate he just combined the two. This would probably have happened sometime before 1230, as on this date there is a reference to

Richard Bigot making gifts to St Algar's, a monastic settlement adjacent to Marston Bigot, so it is likely by then he would have inherited the main estate.[12]

We can assume that Richard Bigot, on succeeding to the vast estate of Marston Bigot, decided to gift the proceeds of his little Oldfield estate to Cirencester Abbey. The mill (almost certainly a flour mill at this time) would have been operated by Alice Panel, not Richard Bigot, so would have either been called Panel's Mill, or, perhaps more likely, Oldfield Mill.

There was now evidence of a small estate called Oldfield of around 100 acres which in the early part of the 13th century had a mill and a house. Given its age and size, Marston Mill House looked to be a good candidate for Richard Bigot's demesne, and it is possible that the mill and the house were next to each other as is now the case. But medieval mills tended to be situated on or very close to the river, so the Marston Mill location, which required a 450 long mill leat to be dug, still didn't make sense.

Researching Oldfield Mill

When searching the Somerset Records Office archive using the term Oldfield Mill, we found some 20 references to maps and deeds dated back as far as 1605, nearly all of which were contained in the Orchardleigh Muniments. Evidently Oldfield Mill, although situated in the Parish of Marston Bigot, had at some point been bought by the Orchardleigh estate.

The first thing we discovered was a beautiful illustrated map of the Orchardleigh estate, dated 1819[13] (*Fig 10*). This showed five mills in this area on the Orchardleigh Estate. From east to west these were:

1   An Iron Mill on the site of Kirty's Mill
2   A flour mill, called White Mill
3   A second Iron Mill which is situated on the site shown as Trehearne Mill on the Dorset & Somerset survey
4   A cloth mill, called Jeffries Mill
5   Adjacent to the charmingly named Eagles Mead, a mill called **Old Field Mill** on the site of Marston Mill

A sixth mill, Sheppard's Mill, is also shown on the map, but this lies outside Orchardleigh.

Looking into the schedule that accompanied this map[14], Old Field Mill was shown as a corn mill let to a Mr William Hopkins. But a deed dated 1824[15] refers to a Soames Mill being let to William Hopkins, and an earlier deed dated 1803, which identifies Kirty's Mill as an iron edge tool mill, and both Jefferies Mill and White Mill as fulling mills[16], refers to there also being a *"... corn grist mill called Soames Mill"*. It therefore appears that the name Soames Mill was also used to describe Old Field Mill.

So we had established that in 1819 Marston Mill was a corn grist mill operated by Hopkins called Old Field Mill, that in 1803 it was called Soames Mill, and that in 1795 it seems to have been referred to as Mr Cookes Mill.

Fig 10   1819 Map of the Orchardleigh estate

Earlier than this all references to flour mills or corn grist mills seem to vanish, but a deed in 1754[17] mentions that Joseph Jefferys (or Jeffries) leased a mill and house in Oldfield, and a 1720 deed[18] refers to there being **two** fulling mills in Oldfield, Marston Bigot.   Sadly this deed mentions no tenants' names, but a 1713 deed[19] states that Susannah Jeffries (Joseph Jeffries wife and daughter of Francis Joyce), leased a farm house and fulling mill in Oldfield from the Champneys, and refers to an original 1704 lease to Francis Joyce and Joseph Jeffries (deceased), both fullers.

This was somewhat confusing, as the 1713 deed says Joseph Jeffries is deceased, yet he seems to have taken out a lease in 1754!   The answer is probably that the Joseph Jeffries who took out the 1754 lease was Susannah Jeffries son. We assume he would also have been a fuller, but since there seem to have been two fulling mills in Oldfield we cannot tell for sure if this lease was for Oldfield Mill or a fulling mill on the site of Jeffries Mill.   However, as far as we can tell ours was the only **house** in Oldfield, and it looks like Jeffries was probably the tenant. That said, the 1819 map shows a house in Bradford Bridge (outside Orchardleigh) being labelled as Mr Jeffries House, and the schedule of the same map shows Mr Jeffries as leasing only one fulling mill (Jeffries Mill) and pasture from Orchardleigh.   So it looks like Jeffries, between 1754 and 1819, sold or sublet the lease to our house and built himself a new house in the village of Bradford Bridge.

Bearing in mind that White Mill (also a fulling mill at this time) was outside Marston Bigot, the conclusion we can draw is that in 1720 our mill, referred to as Oldfield Mill, was a fulling mill not a flour mill.   This idea is reinforced by a 1656 indenture by Honor Champneys of a tenement (i.e. a house) and a tucking mill (another name for fulling mill) lying in 'Oldfeild' (sic). This was leased to John Joyce and his two sons John and Francis *"... for rent £3 (a quarter) plus 2 capons at the feast of the circumcision of Christ and 2 days work all Harvest"*.[20] The indenture itself cites an earlier lease in the *"... 5th year of Charles first"* (1630) to John Joyce. Finally, a marriage settlement between John Champneys and Honor Chaldecott in 1605 mentions *"...two fullinge mills in Oldfielde within the pishe (parish) of Marston Bigott alias Marston Bigood..."*[21] Once again it does not specify to whom they were let.

There are no Orchardleigh deeds earlier than 1605, but another clue is provided by Leyland, who wrote in 1540:

> *"... and 'about 2 myles off I cam to a Botome, where there an other Broke ran into Frome. And in this Botome dwell certain good clothiars havynge fayre Howsys and Tukkynge Myles'.*[22]

McGarvie concludes that this is a reference to Spring Gardens, where the Mells Brook joins the Frome.[23] So this confirms that there was more than one tucking mill in the area as early as 1540, and that our house was probably described as a 'fayre Howse'.

But that still didn't solve the issue of our mill being sited so far from the river. Furthermore, tucking or fulling mills were incredibly noisy affairs, requiring the cloth to be continuously pounded with water-driven hammers to felt it and improve its quality. They were definitely not the sort of thing you would want situated right next to your fair house: a contemporary example is Iford Manor, near Bradford on Avon, which is sited about 200 yards away from the fulling mill which brought such immense wealth to John Horton in the early 16th century.

Fulling mills were extremely good business. Ken Rogers states *"The possession of a fulling mill was clearly desirable enough to prompt clothiers to establish new ones if they could"*.[24] So an explanation might be that both the leat and mill building sited adjacent to our house might have been built when there was a boom in building fulling mills, and people would have been prepared to invest the substantial sum necessary to dig out a 450 yard long leat. Prior to this Marston Mill would simply have been the site of a dwelling house, and Alice Panel's flour mill would have been elsewhere on the estate. That explains why the site is set so far back from the river: a dwelling house would need to be close enough to the river for water and fishing, but sufficiently distant to prevent it being flooded.

There were now two new questions to answer: first, was there anywhere close to our house that might have been the site of a medieval mill, and second, was there any sign of a structure at Marston Mill which might date back to the 13th century?

Further Evidence from Marston Mill House.

We were fairly sure that Marston Mill House was in former times a 70' long residence, however, looking the length of the building along the main upstairs corridor, (*Fig 11*) it is clear that the long northern wall is not straight, but is bent at the point of the main central fireplace stack. In other words the house is very slightly broader at the centre, and tapers at either end. This suggested the possibility that the house was not built as a single 70' long two storey dwelling, but rather that the eastern half might have had a different function to the western half.

The bend in the northern wall might be movement. However, examination of the outside of the northern wall reveals no sign of the wall leaning outwards, and shows clearly the same bend in the wall as is visible inside. But even more interesting is that there is another anomaly in this wall: a 4' high line of quoins located exactly at the point where the central chimney stack is built (*Fig 12*). Being situated next to a solid stone chimney stack means these cannot have been the edge of a window, but they are located exactly at the centre of the house, where the western section would have ended. The quoins are about 2' lower than the full height of the house, which, judging by the stonework, has been increased in height along the whole of the length of the western section.

Fig 11 Bend in upper corridor suggesting a house built in two sections

Fig 12 Line of quoins in north wall adjacent to central chimney stack

The top of this line of quoins is 13' above the ground, and the line seems to run down to about 5' above ground. At this point there is a plinth (a line of horizontal stones) which runs the whole 27' length of the eastern section. So now we had an indication of a building to the west of the central fireplace, measuring 42' x 21', with walls around 13' high, and to the east of this a 27' long extension with walls only 5' high.

This meant that the large chimney with the 1507 bressumer beam at the centre of the house, which faces east, would have been an **addition** to the original western building. In other words, the western section of the building is the older of the two halves, and predates 1507.

Thirteen feet is not very high for the walls of a two storey building, but further examination shows that this older western section was almost certainly a single storey hall. Visible in the western gable is the outline of a filled-in curved-topped window opening about 4'6" high (*Fig 13*). It is too small to be a door, and the cill of this window opening is about the same level as the first floor of the house, which means it was not a first floor window. Instead it appears to be a window set about 7' above the inside ground floor level. Since medieval people didn't like windows to be low enough for people outside to look in, this is roughly where you would expect a window to be if it were illuminating a single storey hall with walls around 13' high.

Fig 13 Curved-topped window opening in western gable.

This western gable also shows an older roof line within the existing stone, pitched at 52°; and inside the house, embedded in the back (western side) of the 1507 chimney stack, is a redundant roof truss with a matching pitch of 51° (*Fig 14*). The significance of sharp roof pitches is that they tended to be used in medieval times to throw more weight vertically onto the wall and less onto the horizontal cross-beams. This reinforces the conclusion that the western section is much older than the eastern part of the building. It also explains why, if the overall ridge height was the same, the walls would have been lower than the current walls.

Dendrochronology has been attempted on this older roof truss, but, as with the ceiling beams, it is made of fast-growing oak, and no clear date could be established. But it does seem certain that this truss predates the central chimney stack. Firstly, had it originally been embedded in the wall as a wall plate it would not have needed any collars to tie it together; secondly, were it a wall plate it would probably have been slow-growing oak, like the other wall plates, not fast-growing oak.

Fig 14 Sharply pitched redundant roof truss situated on the western side of the centre chimney stack. The bottom collar of the truss is in the wall of the bedroom below.

This roof truss has now been fully exposed, and comprises two substantial struts tied at the centre and at the bottom with collars. Within the truss are remains of some sort of wattle structure, the function of which is not clear. The lower collar, which is embedded in the wall of the bedroom below, is set at the same level as the top of the quoins in the outside north wall. This made it too low to walk under at first floor level, so when a first floor was installed in the single storey western hall area, most of the lower half of the purlin on the right side was cut out to allow access between the western and eastern halves of the building (*Fig 15*). Had this been a live truss at the time and not embedded in the fireplace, it would inevitably have collapsed, so the truss was never active as part of a two storey building.

Fig 15 Lower collar with end cut out to allow first floor

Some further evidence has emerged recently to give an idea of the date of this part of the building. During the construction of the soakaway we found that the foundations of the 1747 wall were actually higher than the inside floor level, and were built on top of an older set of foundations (*Fig 16*). These earlier foundations extend 18" further down (8" below the original internal floor level), have their own plinth, and appear to be resting on the natural clay and packed stone substrate.

Adjacent to these ancient foundations was a retaining wall about 20" away, which presumably was built because the land to the south was higher. A large number of pottery finds have been recovered from the ditch between the foundations and the retaining wall; but perhaps most interesting is a pottery jug handle, found in the soil behind the retaining wall (*Fig 17*). This has oblique knife slashes along its length, which Alan Vince identifies as a feature of pottery in the 13th century.[25] This has been confirmed by medieval pottery expert Lorraine Mepham to be likely to date from the 13th century, probably made at the Crockerton Pottery near Warminster[26]. This indicates that the retaining wall, and presumably the barn foundations, date back at least to sometime in the 1200s.

Fig 16 Older medieval foundations below wall re-faced in 1747.

Fig 17 Knife-slashed jug handle dated to 13th century.

It now looks certain that the western building of Marston Mill House is a single-storey medieval hall house that dates back at least to the 13th century. It may have been thatched or have had a stone roof, but it would almost certainly have had a central fireplace with a smoke vent above, possibly burning on the huge smoke-stained flagstone found below the present sitting room floor. Around 1220 this hall house would have housed Richard of Aldfeld and his retainers, and the single storey eastern building would probably have housed his animals. An outline drawing of what Oldfield Hall might have looked like is shown in *Fig 18*, showing the hall in black, the parts still in situ (window, truss, ashlar, door, and plinth) in red, and the eastern barn in blue. This drawing is set against an old black & white aerial photograph of Marston Mill House before the woods were planted.

In the absence of any woodwork or carved stone, there is nothing to indicate the exact date for this old hall. It may have been a building built especially for Richard Bigot, but Michael McGarvie speculates that it may equally have been the original home of the Bigots, and was lived in by the younger brother after the others left for the much larger Marston Bigot estate. So how and why did the estate get the name Oldfield?

Oldfield Hall c 1200
Attached Barn
Visible Features

Fig 18 Marston Mill in the 19ᵗʰ century showing the outline of 13ᵗʰ century Oldfield Hall (photograph provenance unknown).

There may be a clue from an earlier reference to Spring Gardens in connection with the Marston Estate: in 1160, Odo FitzRichard, then Lord of the Manor of Marston, is recorded as having gifted the tithes of a Marston parishioner called 'Robert of Buckland' to Cirencester Abbey. McGarvie believes that this Robert of Buckland's holding, which would have been near to Buckland Dinham, was probably in Spring Gardens.[27] Given the repeated use of the name Richard and Robert in the Bigot family (the first Bigot to hold Marston was a Richard, his son was Robert, and his brother Richard) it is possible that this Robert of Buckland was himself a member of a branch of the Bigot family, whose increasing influence enabled his son Richard to acquire the Manor of Marston off the FitzRichards?

This would mean our house might well have been built and lived in by Robert of Buckland, as early as the middle of the 12ᵗʰ century, and this would explain its being referred to as Aldfeld. The old English etymology of Feld (i.e. Field) is *"A plain, pasture, open land, cultivated land as opposed to woodland."* If a branch of the Bigots had originally settled in and built a house on the land surrounding Marston Mill before 1160, then it is quite likely that they would refer to this as being their 'Old Field', thus Richard 2, younger brother of Robert, would have been residing in Aldfeld, meaning the Old Field where the Bigot family originally lived.

Medieval Oldfield Mill

If Marston Mill House was originally a 12th or 13th century hall house, it does not seem very likely it would have had the mill attached to it. Firstly, it would have needed a very large number of men working for a very long time to dig the 450 yard leat through solid limestone; secondly, in 1225, the mill was operated by Peter Panel's daughter, Alice, which suggests a separate establishment; thirdly, given that Oldfield Hall would probably have had its main elevation on the north side (medieval buildings usually faced north so as to avoid the warm winds that were thought to blow the plague from the south) the presence of a mill would have greatly inconvenienced the Bigots, effectively reducing the front of their hall to an industrial site.

So the next task was to see if there was a more likely site for the medieval Oldfield Mill. It must have been on or near to the river, and somewhere near Marston Mill House. We knew that there were two fulling mills in Oldfield, and that one of them in later years was owned by Jeffries and presumably called Jeffries Mill. So is there any sign of a second defunct mill on a site near to Marston Mill House? Indeed, there is, at Five Hatches.

Five Hatches lies on a sharp bend in the Mells Brook. It is situated north-east of Marston Mill, and labelled on the 1886 Ordnance Survey map as 'Sluice' (*Fig 8*). The name comes from when there were five sluice gates that could be closed to allow water to run along a canal to irrigate the fields to the east at Longhouse Farm. It is only about 170 yards from Marston Mill House, and the river banks upstream of Five Hatches are higher than downstream by 7' or more. This means the water level on the upstream side of Five Hatches was 7' higher than downstream, as would be expected on a mill site. There is also a widened area of river upstream of where the hatches were, which looks like a millpond (*Fig 19*).

But what is most unusual about this site is its size and construction. It covers an area of at least 500 square feet, and has been built with massive dressed stones, some as big as 5' x 2' (*Fig 20*). The hatches have been cut into an existing 18' wide 'U' shaped structure extending some 30' along the river bed, the floor of which is built of high quality dressed flagstones. This is in stark contrast to the other sluices, which are simply bedded into a single course of stone blocks lining the riverbank. Why spend all this money and effort creating a structure of this size and quality whose function is ostensibly just to irrigate fields downstream? It seems much more likely that this is the site of a disused mill.

A visit by members of the Bath & Camerton Archaeological Society revealed further evidence, in the form of a huge number of partially buried dressed limestone blocks lying right next to where the mill building would have stood. Since the new leat and race arrangement would have cut this area off from road access, these very large blocks must have come from the demolition of a substantial building already in place on the river and in general the only large buildings built on rivers were mills.

Fig 19 Possible millpond at Five Hatches.

Fig 20 Five Hatches showing massive stones used in construction, with dressed stone floor visible below the water.

Some further evidence of the possible location of Oldfield Mill at Five Hatches has been found using LIDAR, an aerial radar system that exposes the contours of the ground beneath vegetation. This shows what looks like a trackway leading from Marston Mill in the direction of the Frome – Buckland Dinham road. The track passes Marston Mill to the south, and then bends north heading directly across the new mill race towards Five Hatches. Crossing the Mells Brook at Murtry Bridge, this track would be the most direct route from Buckland Dinham to Oldfield Mill.

So the site in the early part of the 12th /13th century looks like this: a mill to the east at Five Hatches, while across the river to the north there is a wooden hovel for farm workers, where Brookover Farm is now. At the centre, with views across all of their land, is a large single room stone hall house for the Bigots and their servants and retainers, with an attached barn for their animals. This would accord with the present Marston Mill site, set well back from the river, yet close enough for fishing and for water to be collected.

The later history of Oldfield Hall

We can assume from his gift to Cirencester Abbey that Richard Bigot left his hall house in the old field when he inherited the Manor of Marston Bigot early in the 13th century. There seem to be no records of who occupied Oldfield over the next three centuries, but at some point the hall had a side chimney stack added to the northern wall, with some sort of stone fireplace inside. We know that in 1507 a very large fireplace was built at the eastern end of the hall (facing east), with a beamed ceiling. This large fireplace was probably for a kitchen, which is supported by the finds in the medieval foundation trench of lots of pottery, some very thin diamond-shaped window glass and a large number of animal bones, all of which point to this being below what was a kitchen window.

There are clear signs of a partition having been set into the easternmost ceiling beam, so this kitchen would have measured about 15' x 14', with another room beyond (perhaps a scullery) measuring 12' x 14'. The room above would have been a Great Chamber (i.e. bedroom). The great chamber had its own chimney in the eastern gable, supported on an elegantly carved stone corbel, still in-situ. There is also a suggestion from a relatively large size first floor opening in the eastern gable wall that this great chamber might have been accessed by an external stone staircase running across the eastern gable. (*Fig 21*)

At the same time as the new kitchen and great chamber were built, there are signs that a 3'6" wide single storey cross-passage may have been installed behind the new kitchen chimney. This would have been entered from the northern (river) side, would have sealed the hall from draughts, and might even have enabled the occupants of the great chamber to observe the proceedings in the hall from a squint or a first floor gallery above the passage.

Fig 21 First floor opening to external staircase

So who was living in this fine house when it was extended in 1507 to boast a hall with a stone fireplace on the side, a cross passage, a kitchen with a large fireplace, and a great chamber above? The Bigots were long gone by this time, having forfeited the estate at the start of the 14th century by *"... fortifying (their) Mansion without license and disrespecting the king's messenger"*, thus incurring the displeasure of King Edward II.[28] The estate eventually passed to the Stourton family, and between 1487 and 1523 the title of Marston Bigot was held by William, 5th Baron Stourton[29]; but it is extremely unlikely that he would have lived in such a relatively small house so far from the main portion of his grand estate. Much more likely is that it was let to one of the clothiers mentioned by Leyland in 1540, and, given that we know that in 1630 a tenement and tucking mill lying in 'Oldfeild' was leased by the Champneys to John Joyce, it could have been one of Joyce's ancestors.

Regarding the freehold ownership of Oldfield, the Champneys of Orchardleigh certainly acquired the estate sometime before 1605, but we have not been able to confirm that they owned it in 1543, as mentioned in the sale particulars. It is possible the Oldfield estate was still entailed to Cirencester Abbey, in which case it would have been acquired by the Crown when the monasteries were dissolved between 1536 and

1538 and the interest might then have been sold on to Orchardleigh. But unless Marston Bigot had disposed of the Oldfield freehold it would still have been their property, even if let to Cirencester Abbey or Orchardleigh. There is no evidence they were short of money around this time, as William 7th Earl of Stourton bought Monksham from the Crown in 1544[30]. Perhaps it is more likely that Orchardleigh, having already acquired the lease from the crown, bought the freehold in 1557? After all, this is the year when the incumbent Lord Stourton was executed in Salisbury for the murder of William Hartgill, and the Marston Bigot estate was (once again) confiscated by the Crown[31]!

Further Developments

At some stage the priorities for the site changed from residential to industrial. A new 450 yard purpose-built leat was dug across Eagle's Mead, and a large single storey mill was built at right-angles to the eastern end of the house.

It is important to stress what a huge investment this must have been. The foundations of the original Oldfield Hall rest on clay with packed limestone on limestone boulders. The leat is around 7' deep and is dug right down into the layer of clay and packed limestone, and the 170 yard mill race is about 4' deeper. Digging it out would have been a massive job: to give some idea, it took two men four hours to dig out a 4' square soakaway just two feet into the packed clay and limestone, so a team of eight men working at the same rate might have taken two years to complete the whole job. The commercial returns would have needed to be very high to justify this amount of work.

Added to the problem would have been what to do with the stones dug out from the leat and race. It looks very likely that the solution was to use these to construct a 250-yard-long elevated drive to the site. This driveway crosses the meadows on a causeway raised between 3' and 5', and runs right up to meet the wall of the mill building at a height about 5' above the internal floor level, not far below the current first floor.

Aside from using up the stone, what did this driveway add to the site? One great benefit would have been to reduce the risk of the mill being cut off by flooding. Even though it is sited 100 yards away from the river, the ground floor of the mill is even now often threatened by flooding. This is a perennial problem with all mills, which require water to be brought up to the building at a level much higher than it leaves. Whoever decided to spend the vast amount of money digging out the leat and building the new mill probably thought they should ensure that the mill could easily be reached, whatever the water level.

What is certain is that the mill installation would have ruined the 'fayre howse' Leland spoke of. The medieval hall would have become part of the mill, with half of the southern frontage buried by the new driveway; the original access to the north, where the main front of the house used to be, would have had the mill race cut across it, and the noise of the fulling mill stocks pounding away would have ruined the tranquillity of the site. So a decision must have been made that the business potential far outweighed the residential value.

For this reason, we believe that the digging of the leat and the building of the mill must have coincided with the 1747 renovation of the house. This was during the peak of mill building in this area, when the opportunity to build a substantial new fulling mill might have been seen as a seriously attractive commercial proposition.

The new mill would have reduced the size of the existing house to being just a kitchen, scullery, and great chamber, certainly not enough accommodation to be of any use. The 1747 renovation of the house compensated for the loss of the old hall by enlarging the remainder of the building to four bedrooms and two reception rooms. The two rooms on the ground floor were entered by a new front door facing south, with an elegant canopy (*Fig 22*); and the four bedrooms were reached by a new semi-circular staircase tower on the north wall (*see Fig 2*). This staircase gave access to the first floor great chamber, now two bedrooms, and two more attic rooms in a new second floor. The old kitchen fireplace in what was now the sitting room was reduced to 4'6", and the bressumer and ceiling beams plastered over as was the fashion in Georgian times. The discovery of the diamond-shaped window glass in the trench confirms that the old leaded lights were replaced by new Georgian windows.

Fig 22 1747 miller's house, showing new door with Georgian canopy and asymmetrical ground floor windows.

One anomaly which lends support to the idea that the house renovation and mill building were coincident, is the thickness of the walls in the western end of the southern elevation of the house. These are around 36" at the ground floor, narrowing to 26" at the first floor. This contrasts with walls around 23" – 26" thick on the eastern end of the house. At first we thought this might be because this was part of the earlier hall building, but further consideration suggests the wall was thickened up as a direct result of the weight of stone and soil resulting from the construction of the elevated driveway: quite simply the pressure the stones placed on the western end of the southern elevation necessitated its reinforcement with a second skin of stone. Evidence of this second skin comes from the old roof line in the western gable, which seems to end about 9" short of the existing walls, and a window opening in the southern elevation which seems to be set back by around 9".

Further evidence that the southern face was increased in thickness came from the excavation of the medieval foundations. We found that the foundations of the 1747 wall were built on top of an older set of foundations (*Fig 16*). What is astonishing is that the 1747 foundations project out over the medieval foundations, with the front 4" of stone effectively resting on nothing. This is exactly what would happen if an extra course of stones were added to the front elevation.

What is also fascinating about this 1747 rebuilt wall is how it reflects the Georgian fixation with symmetry. The original southern wall of the 13th century barn was not only 4" further back, but was tapered, as was the northern wall, making the building narrower at the eastern end. When the kitchen and great chamber were added in 1507 this tapered line was maintained: the southern wall was the back of the building, and so it did not matter if it had a bend in it. But with the 1747 renovation the southern wall became the front of the building, and a bend was not acceptable to the builders. In order to ensure that the southern face of the whole building was straight they rebuilt the eastern wall in line with the western wall.

We know this because of the bedding of the ceiling beams in what was the kitchen, and now became the new sitting room. The beam closest to the bressumer fireplace is bedded into the wall up to the point of the 'stop', or widened end, of the beam (*Fig 23*), however, the end of the stop of the next beam along is 7 inches away from the wall, indicating that the wall had been rebuilt wider at this point (*Fig 24*). The final beam furthest from the fireplace only just reaches the wall, being a full 12" out of position: it is only prevented from dropping by a 9" wooden corbel set into the wall (*Fig 25*). All these beams would have been plastered over, but it is a small miracle that the entire first floor did not collapse! This alteration of the position of the wall, which compromised the internal structural integrity of the entire building, seems to have been done simply in order to ensure the wall was in a straight line.

Fig 23 Beam with stop against wall   *Fig 24 Beam with stop 6" from wall*   *Fig 25 Beam out of wall, on corbel*

There is another indication of how symmetry was much more important than structural integrity in Georgian times. The windows either side of the door clearly needed to be three lights wide and exactly symmetrical with each other and the door, so the window opening nearest the fireplace was built right up to the point at which the beam in *Fig 23* was meant to be supported by the wall. This weakened the support for the beam, as at some later date the window opening was narrowed and the window made deeper. The remnant of the old wider and shallower window opening which matches the window on the other side of the door can be seen in *Fig 22*, as can the narrower asymmetrical window, installed to stop the beam from collapsing.

We can guess that if the renovation and mill building took place together in 1747 that it was probably carried out by Joseph Jeffries, who would have inherited the lease from his mother Susannah. Jeffries, if he was operating two fulling mills, would have accumulated a lot of money by the mid-18th century, and we know that most of the adjacent mills in 1747 were either fulling mills or edge tool mills, and business in both of these trades was still booming. It looks most likely that he decided to invest his money in replacing or supplementing the smaller of their two fulling mills with a grand larger one on our site.

Evidence in favour of this is the size of Marston Mill, which is very large for a corn mill, but about right for a fulling mill. Ken Rogers says, *"Even when water mill sites were most eagerly sought after (for the woollen trade), the value of grist mills, especially when they were situated near towns, remained high enough to prevent the wholesale conversion of them all to cloth mills."*[32] Since the other ancient corn mill near Frome, White Mill, was by now a fulling mill, it seems quite possible that Jeffries recognised the opportunity for a brand new mill that both fulled cloth <u>and</u> ground corn.

We think it unlikely that the original Oldfield fulling mill carried on operating after 1747. If it was situated at Five Hatches, the new mill would have robbed it of water, and the new mill race would have made access from the south impossible. Our guess is that before 1747 it was abandoned, and the stone used elsewhere, but all we know for certain is that in 1863 a set of five sluices was installed there to irrigate the fields downstream.

Sometime before 1795 Jeffries had moved out of the miller's cottage on our site (assuming he ever lived in it) and either sold his lease or sublet our mill to a Mr Cooke, and after him a Mr Soames. He would probably have used the proceeds to expand the other fulling mill in Oldfield into a fair-size cloth factory (Jeffries Mill), and to build himself a new house in nearby Bradford Bridge, which would have been a lot more pleasant than noisy Spring Gardens. Certainly the schedule of the 1819 Orchardleigh map shows him leasing just one mill, and the map shows a house called Jeffries House, on the corner of Jeffries Lane and Coalash Lane. This house is still there, now called Hurst.

An 1820 Orchardleigh inventory shows Old Field Mill classified as a 'factory and flour mill', and let to Mr Hopkins, along with a house and some land (*Fig 26*). As we observed already, the 'factory' would have been around 70' x 25', but the 1819 map (*Fig 10*) shows another detached building to the north, running along the leat at the back of the miller's cottage. Ken Rogers speculates that this might originally have been the flour milling part. It would certainly have further diminished the habitability of the house, a testament to which is the fact that the map shows Hopkins had built himself a new house at the start of the elevated driveway, now called Mill Cottage.

We know that the flour mill was a great success: by 1886 the Ordnance Survey map shows the building to the north had been expanded and attached to the house, and a stone barn, still in situ, had been erected to the south (*Fig 8*). The walls of the mill were raised at some stage by 4' to incorporate a full-length grain storage floor, and in 1899 a brand new Gilkes vertical flume-fed turbine was installed, driving three mill wheels, and at some point, a 40' extension was built to the east of the house, incorporating a stable, and taking it to its full 115' length.

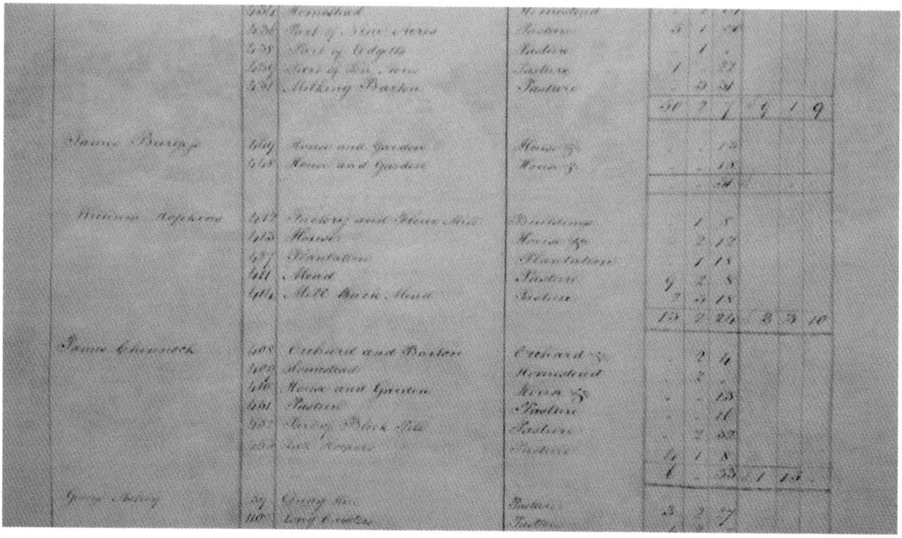

Fig 26 1821 Orchardleigh Map Schedule

Finally, after perhaps 230 years grinding grain, Marston Mill, the last of the six mills in Spring Gardens still operating, itself became a victim of changing times. Business was still good, and towards the end, the 75-year-old owner Bill Ellis was reputedly grinding and mixing dog food. But an article in the Somerset Guardian / Standard on August 8th 1975 declared *"There's trouble down at the mill"*, and the drought, apparently worse than in 1921, was *"... causing Bill's Mill to come to a grinding halt."* This was despite the removal of one of the three millstones and the installation of a Lister diesel engine. The mill was put up for auction as a going concern, but after finding no buyers, and a second disastrous drought in 1976, it ceased operating and was sold. It was eventually bought by Tim Heneage, who ironically converted it back to a dwelling house, as it had been more than 800 years earlier.

Summary

At the end of our investigation, we believe the timeline for the development of the Marston Mill site is as follows:

1   An area of woodland owned by the Marston Estate in present-day Spring Gardens was cleared sometime in the 11th or 12th century, and in 1160 it was rented by Robert of Buckland. At some point a stone hall with a barn was erected on it and a flour mill built nearby on the river Mells, at Five Hatches.

2   Around 1180, Richard le Bigod, possibly Robert of Buckland's son, managed to get possession of the nearby Marston Estate. When he moved there he left some members of his family living in their previous home, which was referred to as Aldfeld (The Old Field.)

3   By the start of the 13th century Aldfeld was occupied by Richard Bigot, younger brother of Robert Bigot, and the mill was operated by Peter Panel.

4   Sometime between 1225 and 1233 Richard Bigot inherited the Marston Bigot Estate from his childless brother Robert. He moved out, giving the proceeds of the Aldfeld estate to Cirencester Abbey. At this time Alice Panel was operating the mill.

5   At some point a chimney stack was added to the north elevation. This may have coincided with the enlargement of the house in 1507 by a clothier. The renovation involved the rebuilding of the barn into a kitchen and scullery with a Great Chamber above, and coincided with the construction of a fulling mill on the Five Hatches flour mill site.

6   In 1540 Leyland visited the site and described it as a 'fayre howse.'

7   At some point before 1605 the freehold of Oldfield and its two fulling mills was acquired by Orchardleigh, and in 1630 a lease for the fulling mill and house was made to John Joyce. The lease passed to his sons John and Francis Joyce in 1656.

8   Francis Joyce was still the leaseholder in 1704, by now sharing the lease with Joseph Jeffries. By 1713 Joyce and Jeffries, both fullers, were dead, and the lease passed to Susannah Jeffries, Francis Joyce's daughter and Joseph Jeffries' wife. At this point the house was referred to as a farm and the mill as a fulling mill.

9   The dwelling house was substantially refurbished in 1747, possibly by Joseph Jeffries, Susannah Jeffries' son. A new leat was dug across Eagles Mead, a new elevated driveway built across the fields in front with the spoil, and a new purpose-built fulling mill erected, attached to the old medieval hall which was incorporated into it. The remainder of the building became a three storey Georgian miller's house with an external staircase tower.

10 In 1795 the mill was being operated by and leased to a Mr Cooke, and after him to a Mr Soames.

11 By 1819 Old Field Mill (sic) was leased to a William Hopkins. An additional building had been erected to the north of the house, and in 1820 the site was described as a 'Factory and Flour Mill'.

12 Sometime before 1863 the mill became known as Marston Mill.

13 By 1885 the buildings to the north of the miller's house had been expanded and attached to the main mill building, and a detached barn for horses and carts had been built to the south.

14 Sometime after this a single storey stable extension was built on the eastern end taking the building to 115' in length.

15 In 1899 there was a major refurbishment to the mill. A new turbine was installed by Gilkes driving three mill wheels. At this point we think the buildings to the north of the miller's house were demolished, and the mill building was expanded upwards to accommodate a full-length grain floor.

16 Finally, following the droughts of 1975 and 1976, the mill, now owned and operated by the Ellis family, went out of business, and the property reverted to being a dwelling house in 1977.

Some of this is fact, and some speculation. Reviewing the evidence, there is a strong indication that Marston Mill conceals a Hall House significantly older than 1507. This lies on the site of a mill which in 1819 was called Old Field Mill, in an area known as Oldfield, and in 1225 Oldfield (or Aldfeld) was home to Richard Bigot, and had a mill. But as yet, other than a pottery jug handle, there is nothing to prove that the parts of the Hall that remain at Marston Mill House date back to the 12th or 13th century, nor is there any hard evidence that the original Oldfield Mill was at Five Hatches. A programme of archaeological investigation is proposed for 2016 which we hope might answer both these questions.

There are other important unanswered questions. For example, we do not know if Richard Bigot was Robert of Buckland's son, nor the identity of the clothier who refurbished and extended the hall in 1507, nor when the freehold of Oldfield passed from Marston Bigot to the Champneys of Orchardleigh, and we do not know for certain that it was Joseph Jeffries who was the lessee who extended the property in 1747.

Any assistance from readers in shedding light on these matters would be greatly appreciated.

[1] Michael McGarvie, The Book of Frome , 28, Barracuda Books, 1980
[2] The Book of Frome ,112
[3] Rev J Collinson, History of Somerset, 216, 1791
[4] The Book of Frome ,110
[5] The Book of Frome ,112
[6] Robin Thornes, Men of Iron,52, FSLS, 2010
[7] K H Rogers, Wiltshire and Somerset Woollen Mills, 207, Pasold, 1976
[8] Somerset Heritage Centre Qrup12 1795

[9] Michael McGarvie, The Book of Marston Bigot, 17, Barracuda Books, 1987

[10] The Book of Marston Bigot, 15

[11] The Book of Marston Bigot, 28

[12] The Book of Frome, 37

[13] Somerset Heritage Centre DD\DU/70

[14] Somerset Heritage Centre DD\DU/86

[15] Somerset Heritage Centre DD\BR\u/10

[16] Somerset Heritage Centre DD\DU/3

[17] Somerset Heritage Centre DD\DU/37

[18] Somerset Heritage Centre DD\DU/1

[19] Somerset Heritage Centre DD\DU/36

[20] Somerset Heritage Centre DD\DU/33

[21] Somerset Heritage Centre DD\SOG/752

[22] Somersetshire Archaeological and Natural History Society's Proceedings 1887, 129

[23] The Book of Frome, 67

[24] Wiltshire & Somerset Woollen Mills,7

[25] A Vince, Assessment of the pottery from an excavation at Dursley, Gloucestershire (PSD03), 2003

[26] Lorraine Mepham, Personal Communication

[27] The Book of Marston Bigot, 27

[28] The Book of Marston Bigot, 29

[29] The History of the Noble House of Stourton in the County of Wilts, 243

[30] The Book of Marston Bigot, 30

[31] The Book of Marston Bigot, 34

[32] Wiltshire and Somerset Woollen Mills, 34

The causeway leading to Marston Mill in winter

Bishop Ken and the Non-Jurors
by John Jolliffe

English life in the second half of the 17th century divides into two sharply contrasting periods. The first, the Puritan regime of Oliver Cromwell, sought to destroy the liturgy of the Church of England, the backbone of most people's devotional life. It made the theatre illegal and abolished the feast of Christmas. It also destroyed a great deal of the treasure of glass and stone at the heart of the nation's churches and cathedrals.

Thomas Ken painted by F Scheffer

The reaction to such iconoclasm was confirmed by the Restoration of Charles II on his 30th birthday in 1660 and with the laxity and license of his behaviour. Between these two extremes there were cases of devotion to high principles. One example was the stand taken on two separate occasions by the Non-Juror clergy, led by the bishops, who refused first to order James II's Declaration of Faith to be read out in their dioceses, as instructed by the king; and then declined, shortly afterwards, to swear allegiance to William III as Supreme Governor of the Church of England, on the grounds that they had previously taken that oath in favour of James, however much they disliked his attempt to impose Roman Catholicism on the country. Thomas Ken, Bishop of Bath and Wells, had stood at James' right hand at his coronation in April 1685. Like Pontius Pilate in rather different circumstances, the bishops' line was *Quod scripsi, scripsi* (What I have written, I have written); or, in this case, *Quod juravi, juravi* (What I have sworn, I have sworn).

Their first crisis had arisen in April 1687, when James issued his Declaration of Indulgence. In theory this was a liberal - and liberating - pronouncement, reversing the penal laws against religions other than the Church of England. Its real purpose, however, was to facilitate the pre-eminence of the Roman Catholic Church. At first, addresses of thanks poured into Whitehall from Quakers, Anabaptists and other non-conforming bodies.

Far stronger was the realisation that James was setting aside, arbitrarily, the anti-Catholic Test Act, passed by Parliament as the cornerstone of religious policy. Many could see that this was likely to lead to other measures of an autocratic nature of the kind that had cost the head of James' father, Charles I. It even seemed to be a step towards rule without Parliament.

*This is the original, a copy of which was presented to Rev W J E Bennett[1]

James issued an Order in Council on May 4th, 1687, requiring the bishops to have the Declaration of Indulgence read out in all the churches and chapels in their dioceses. The bishops reacted quickly. Sancroft, Archbishop of Canterbury, led six of them to wait on the king: besides Ken there were Compton (Bishop of London), White (Peterborough), Turner (Ely) and Cartwright (Chester). Their petition stated their conscientious scruples against reading the declaration and begged the king to withdraw it. Ken explained that 'we have two duties to perform, our duty to God and our duty to Your Majesty. We honour you, but we fear God'. James was furious and dismissed them as 'trumpeters of sedition'. The next day a letter was sent to every parish priest in the country urging that the declaration should not be read. The result was overwhelming. In a radius of ten miles of London it was read in only four churches, including Westminster Abbey, where the entire congregation walked out, leaving only the choristers and the scholars of Westminster School behind.

The bishops were then told they would be prosecuted in the Court of King's Bench and 'must enter recognizances to appear'. This they declined to do, on the grounds that, as members of the House of Lords, they were under no obligation to do so. Nevertheless, the Lord Chancellor, George Jeffreys, later to gain notoriety as the 'hanging judge' at the Bloody Assizes following the Monmouth Rebellion of 1685, ordered the serjeant-at-arms to conduct them as prisoners to the Tower of London. A week later after visits from Lord Clarendon and John Evelyn among others, they were brought to trial in Westminster Hall, with sympathetic crowds cheering them on their way. After the summing up they were allowed to go off to their residences. The jury was locked in for the night and 'were heard at midnight in heated disagreement, and again about 3 am'. At 10 am the foreman gave the verdict of 'Not Guilty' and crowds outside broke out in wild cheering. Church bells rang, guns fired salvoes, bonfires blazed and soon the bishops went home.

Events moved rapidly. By November 6th, 1688 William of Orange was landing an army of 17,000 of whom, ironically, a quarter were Roman Catholics. By the 24th Ken left his diocese to avoid possible contact with the Dutch, some of whom were known to him personally from his unhappy time as chaplain to the child bride Princess Mary in the gloomy court of The Hague back in 1680. Unlike the Vicars of Bray and most of their bishops, Ken remained loyal to the man who had sent him to the Tower of London. But on December 11th, 1688 James fled from Whitehall by night, casting the Great Seal into the Thames.

It is worth looking at the sequence of events that had brought Ken to Wells. After The Hague he was appointed chaplain to the king and when the latter ordered the building of a new palace at Winchester, he was in the habit of lodging at the deanery on his visits. Ken had been installed as a prebendary there in 1669 and the harbinger responsible for the accommodation of the court had wanted Nell Gwyn to be lodged at the prebendary's residence, conveniently close to the deanery.

The Seven Bishops tried for sedition

Ken refused and, instead, more conveniently still, a small apartment was built on to the deanery to house her. In 1685 the Bishop of Winchester had died and the then Bishop of Bath and Wells was appointed in his place. Charles had to find another bishop and he decided to appoint 'the little fellow who refused poor Nelly a lodging'. In 1685, only a week after his consecration as bishop, having already taken the Oath of Allegiance on his election, he ministered to Charles on his deathbed. The custom at the time was for a newly appointed bishop to provide, at his own expense, a banquet for 'the cream of the clergy and nobility'. Ken decided instead to present what the banquet would have cost him to the fund for rebuilding St Paul's Cathedral 'in lieu of his consecration dinner'. Another considerable act of generosity by Ken was his decision to forego the sum of £4,000, which had come to the episcopal treasury from legal dues on the renewal of various leases. This he made over to a collection intended to support Protestant refugees from France, who had fled their country after the Revocation of the Treaty of Nantes. In his few short years at Wells he regularly entertained 12 poor men and women at dinner in the palace. Hardly were these pious acts completed than arose the first crisis of his time at Wells. The Protestant Duke of Monmouth, who had been exiled by his acknowledged father, Charles II, returned with two ships and landed at Lyme Bay in Dorset. Secretary Pepys at the Admiralty seized the vessels and cut off any means of escape for Monmouth by sea. His only option was to fight on land. At first Monmouth was welcomed rapturously by large numbers of Taunton's and Bridgwater's citizens. James' disciplined troops under Louis de Duras, 2nd Earl of Feversham had little trouble in routing Monmouth's rabble of supporters, who were mostly armed with pitchforks, scythes and other agricultural implements. More than 1,300 of them were killed and perhaps as many again captured and found guilty of treason. They were executed on and around the battlefield at Sedgemoor and left to rot. Some of the prisoners were incarcerated in a church in Wells and Ken did what he could to save them from death or transportation and to relieve their families, even forgiving the amateur soldiers for having used the cathedral as stables and terrorising the city. Monmouth was captured, cowering in a ditch, and wrote an abject letter begging James, who he had unwisely described earlier as a usurper, murderer and enemy of religion, to receive him. It did him no good. Ken attended him in his final hours and urged him to repent. At first Monmouth refused, but on being reminded of all the carnage that he had caused among the Somerset 'hobbledehoys' he repented.

On January 28th, 1689 the Commons passed a resolution based on no legal principle: that James 'having withdrawn himself from the Kingdom had abdicated the government, and that the throne had become vacant'. For all they knew James might have changed his mind, rallied his supporters and come back. William declined stubbornly to be in the position of his wife's 'gentleman usher', which as far as England was concerned was what he was, or of being regent or even king consort. Since no alternative could be suggested and his supporters being understandably determined to remain on the best possible terms with him, as well as to feather their nests, he succeeded in bulldozing his way into sharing the throne. When considering William's character, Samuel Johnson's description of it is worth recalling: *Arbitrary, insolent, gloomy, rapacious and brutal... neither in great things nor in small the manners of a gentleman, and only regarded his promise when it was in his interest to keep it.*

Ken's biographer, H A L Rice, while detesting William's character, nevertheless concedes as follows: *In defence of the liberties and independence of small nations, in opposition to over-towering ambition and lust for power, he remained constant, fearless and inflexible.*

It remains an impressive tribute. A dubious resolution declaring the throne vacant by the two Houses of Parliament, in joint session, was passed by just 62 votes to 47, Ken being among the minority. Thirty-seven peers then protested against William and Mary being declared king and queen, 12 of them, including Ken, being bishops. Nevertheless, other measures were passed transferring authority and allegiance from James and, on February 12th, Ken quit the House of Lords, never to enter it again. He refused to abandon his sacred principles long before being asked to swear allegiance to William.

Even in their deprived state, the more extreme bishops still regarded themselves as legitimate holders of their sees while their successors were viewed as intruders and schismatics. Bishop Sancroft died two years later, in 1693, and the extremists, with the approval of James in exile at St Germain, secretly consecrated two more bishops. The Non-Jurors were now suspected of being active supporters of James and were harassed accordingly by the new regime, but no evidence of treasonable intent could be found against them. In 1702 Queen Anne offered to restore Ken, an offer he declined though he accepted a pension. It was not until 1715 that any serious attempt was made to oust what by then was the Hanoverian regime and it soon failed.

Meanwhile, Ken had been given shelter still in his old diocese by his Oxford contemporary, Lord Weymouth, at Longleat in Wiltshire. A few letters of Ken's survive from this period, always beginning with the rather formal opening, 'My very good lord'. Sadly they throw little light on Ken's character, which is anyway illustrated by his impeccable behaviour while still in office. He sold his personal possessions when leaving Wells for over £700, which he handed over to Weymouth in return for an annuity of £80. He kept only his library, which is still at Longleat, the catalogue of which is interesting, both for its contents and for its gaps. It contains no Shakespeare, nor any of the Elizabethan dramatists. No English Reformers are represented; Cranmer and Latimer are absent, as is Luther. Yet there are many works of the Church fathers: Clement of Alexandria, Origen, Tertullian, Eusebius, Gregory Nazianzen, Ambrose, Augustine, Bernard, to mention only some of the better known. More surprisingly there are a number of Roman Catholic notables: a life of St Ignatius, the works of Thomas à Kempis and St Francis de Sales, Mabillon and the Doctrines of Bossuet, as well as the Roman Missal and Breviary. For some reason Ken left a substantial collection of Spanish authors to Bath Abbey, which were recently transferred to the Cathedral Library at Wells. There are also the works of major contemporary thinkers, including Sancroft, Jeremy Taylor, Hobbes and others, and, very surprisingly in view of his underhand and dishonest treatment of Ken, three works by Bishop Gilbert Burnet.

Classical authors are also well represented and although Homer, Herodotus and Aeschylus are absent (perhaps given away to friends?) most of the Greek canon is there, as are the main Latin authors: Horace, Livy, Ovid, Tacitus, Juvenal, Catullus, Cicero, Lucan, Martial and Pliny, probably survivors from Ken's studies at Winchester and Oxford. English authors include Holinshed and Froissart, Bede and Ussher and, among contemporary literature, the works of Milton, Crashaw, Herbert and Donne.

Although Ken was lucky to fall on his feet at Longleat, he was just 54 and a loss to his diocese. His remaining years were spent largely in private study and devotions, mainly in the chapel that was set up for him at Longleat. He also composed a number of undistinguished verses and a few hymns, among them the well-known 'Awake my Soul, and with the Sun'. He is certain to have been troubled by the fate of so many of his fellow clergy on being deprived and to have lamented the loss suffered by the Church of England on their departure. Some of the clergy found employment as private tutors, schoolmasters or domestic chaplains, but this would hardly have been appropriate for Ken, who had held exalted positions both at court and, however briefly, at Wells and who could not bring himself to play any active part in the new ecclesiastical regime. But he certainly gave encouragement and advice over the foundation of Lord Weymouth's Grammar School in Warminster, which still survives as Warminster School. He kept old friendships alive, not least with former colleagues who had taken the Oath of Supremacy and whose consciences Ken respected.

He was not tied down at Longleat. To avoid the house's crowded Christmas celebrations he was in the habit of going to stay with various friends and faithful supporters, including Lord Weymouth's widowed daughter-in-law at Lewesdon near Sherborne and with Dr Cheyney, the headmaster of Winchester, who had once been his chaplain. He also acted as a kind of spiritual director to two maiden ladies, the Misses Kemeys at Portishead. In 1704 he was staying with his nephew, Izaak Walton the younger, in the Rectory at Poulshot, not far from Longleat, when it was badly damaged in a storm described by Defoe. Twelve ships of the line were wrecked and the

Eddystone Lighthouse destroyed. At Wells, part of the Bishop's Palace collapsed on Bishop Kidder and his wife, killing them. It is a supreme irony that this fate befell Ken's successor and not himself. Ken died in 1711 at the age of 74 and was buried in accordance with his instructions in a simple grave outside the church of St John in Frome, at that time the nearest parish church to Longleat.

Bishop Ken's tomb

Principles still at stake

To bring the story of expulsion up to date, another more bitter irony, much resented in the Diocese of Bath and Wells, was the recent high-handed move by the Church Commissioners to prevent the recently installed bishop, the Rt Rev Peter Hancock, from occupying the flat in the Bishop's Palace. This plan was made without consulting the new bishop himself and the commissioners failed to consult the dean. So the new bishop was likely to be deprived of his lodging before even setting foot in it. A former rectory three and a half miles away was bought back at huge cost for him to occupy, thus removing him from the historic centre of the diocese. This appeared to be a purely materialistic move in order to increase the theoretical tourist value of the Bishop's Palace. There was even a strong suspicion, although they may deny it, that the Commissioners would next try to sell off the Bishop's Palace itself. Following a forceful and eloquent letter to the press by a former dean and other robust protests, the Church Commissioners referred the matter to the Archbishop's Council, which sent an envoy to Wells, who investigated the situation and reversed the Commissioners' decision. No doubt they will be more careful in future before trying to betray their solemn obligation to protect the Church's architectural legacy and a fascinating chapter in its history.

[1] *FSLS Yearbook 14, p19, 2011*

This article first appeared in History Today, April 2015 and I am grateful to the editor, Paul Lay, for permission to reprint it. Ed.

Brunswick Place, Fromefield
by Keith Falconer

Brunswick Place 1985   *Photo: Keith Falconer*

Cruse's map of 1813, the first detailed map of Frome, shows Fromefield as a scatter of houses alongside the main road to Bath with a cluster near the junction with Spring Lane but no Brunswick Place. It does show what is now the Garden House, 30 Fromefield, and closer to the town the small cottage which is now 34 Fromefield.

It is not until the Dixon & Maitland survey of 1838 that Brunswick Place is shown. This survey depicts two properties, plots 1599 and 1601, but Brunswick Place, now 31-33 Fromefield, appears to have been built in 1819, by Edward G Pitt a silversmith of Cheap Street, as a three unit terrace, which could be occupied either singly, or as two or three separate properties. In corroboration the Rates books show that it was first owned by E G Pitt until his death in 1850[*], when the owner was named as a Mrs Major at the time of the tenancy of the Rossetti family, although the deeds suggest that a Samuel Trotman actually owned the property from 1853.

* I am indebted to the late Derek Gill whose research discovered that a mortgage of £500 was raised by E G Pitt and his wife Ann to build the property in 1819.

The building is aligned alongside the main Frome to Bath turnpike road half a mile north of Frome Market Place as indicated by a Black Dog Trust milestone across the road. Behind a metre high made-up garden, it presents a three-storey facade to the street over a basement with light wells, but to the rear the lowest level is a sub-basement looking out over the gardens, however, the present appearance would seem to date from remodelling in the 1850s. The property is unusual: each unit has its own main door though only the central property has a door on the frontage thus giving the appearance of a single large house. This door is panelled and set in a round-headed door-case and the flanking

Dixon & Maitland map of Frome 1838 FSLS

properties have similar panelled doors on their side elevations. Internally there are three staircases with similar details but very different arrangements. The staircase to the central house is contained in a stair turret to the rear of the spacious entrance hall while the stair to the northern house is in a stair turret to the side behind a small entrance porch and the stair to the south is against the rear wall off a small entrance hall in the side of the building.

Milestone Photo:
Janet Dowding

The Rate books in Taunton confirm that the terrace was indeed rented out by the non-resident landlord Edward Pitt until 1850 to varying combinations of tenants. Significantly, in 1849, a William Robert Baxter initially rented the two units making up plot 1599, and then, when the ownership changed to Mrs Major in 1850, he rented the whole terrace and ran it as a boarding school. The 1851 census is very detailed and shows that 27 persons were staying in Brunswick Place on the day of the census: the 57 year old Baxter, his wife and their four children, the youngest of whom had been born in the terrace, two young teachers one from Luton the other from Zurich, 16 boarding boy pupils ranging in age from 9 to 16 and three servant girls. Baxter last paid rates in October 1852 and it would seem that the school failed shortly afterwards leaving the whole property vacant and ripe for the Rossetti occupation, when they came in 1853.

When the Rossetti family occupied Brunswick Place, Christina's 'cottage by the Styx', they were the only tenant - as had been William Baxter before them. He had paid a half yearly rental of £40 and £22 for the entire block in two properties but the Rossetti family paid £22 rent for only one of the properties and the garden and it seems that the adjacent property was unoccupied. Thus, although there was inter-communication at more than one level, this rental evidence and

Photo: Keith Falconer

Christina's description of the drawing room and schoolroom would appear to suggest the Rossetti's occupancy focussed on 31 Fromefield.

Immediately upon the Rossettis' departure, the next tenants, and there were three of them, were to pay an increased rent for two properties: £22, £22 and a reduced rent £21 on the third. This sequence of changes in rents 1853-54 would seem to coincide with an enlargement and remodelling of the block for which there is plenty of surviving archaeological evidence and a division of the garden. To the rear of 32 and 33 a block of eight rooms has been added with only inter-communication at the basement level. The original slated roof to the front block survives below the hipped roof of the extension. The present wide eaves to the front elevation are evidenced internally by a change in roof rafters profile and the iron and glass canopy to 32 may also date from this remodelling. The significant change in the ground plan of two houses in the terrace is shown on the 1886 OS map when compared with the 1838 map by Dixon & Maitland.

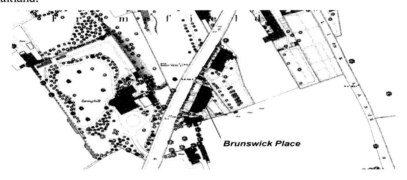

Brunswick Place

A section of the 1886 OS map showing Brunswick Place

The enigma of the painted head.

It seems likely that while the Rossettis were in occupation some extensive building work was in hand, hence the reduction in rent in the second period and, intriguingly perhaps, the availability of new sections of plaster. This introduces a tantalizing possibility!

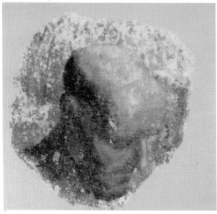

Photo: RCHME James Davies & Keith Falconer

This painted head was revealed during redecoration of 33 Fromefield in the 1970s when wall paper was removed but subsequently obscured until later redecoration in the 1990s. The high quality of the head suggests a more competent artist than a local tradesman and as this section of wall backs on to the 1854 extension when there would be new plaster there is the possibility that it might be a doodle by someone associated with the Rossettis' occupation of the block. Dante Rossetti is known to have only visited Fromefield once, in 1854, while his work on new plaster in the Library of the Oxford Union is some three years later so he would not have been experimenting for that commission. The head was photographed by the RCHME in 1998 but subsequent research into the possible artist was inconclusive.

Brunswick Place – a postscript

Although a Mrs Major is named in the Rate books as owner when the Rossettis were in residence, the deeds show that Samuel Trotman, a local brewer, acquired the properties in 1853 with a mortgage from Betsy Roberts. The Trotman family was to be associated with the terrace, as were several mortgage partners, including Edwin Bush and Rev William Bennett, for much of the rest of the century. Until the close of the 19th century Brunswick Place was sometimes occupied by three tenants, often professionals such as Rev Daniel Anthony, the minister of Zion Congregational Church, but sometimes as a school. One of these episodes impinges on the life of another noted Frome resident: Clara Grant. In the 1870s and 1880s a Miss Cox ran a Seminary for Young Ladies in 32 Fromefield which was immortalised by Clara Grant's scathing description of her five years there in her autobiography, *Farthing Bundles*. There were 6-8 boarders and 15-20 day pupils and the main schoolroom was a small back room while the larger drawing room was only used for interviewing parents. The pupils learnt everything by rote and there was absolutely no scope for intelligence. They were never told that Christina Rossetti had lived next door nor taught any of her poems beloved by children.

Back Schoolroom in 32 Fromefield   *Photo: Keith Falconer*

The deeds show that in the early 20th century the individual freeholds of the three properties were acquired by owners who were to occupy the houses and this has continued to the present day.

FROME - THE PARISH CLOCK

The finishing stroke in the work of restoration at our parish church was given last week, when the town clock, after a silence of four or five years, was brought into working order. The labour involved in the undertaking has been immense, and has taken seven months to complete. The contractor was Mr J W Singer, of Frome, who, being a worker in brass and other metals, as well as a clock-maker, has executed the work in the most thorough manner. The works are principally new, and are of great strength. The pendulum is two cwt, the hour weight six cwt, the quarters weight three cwt, and the chimes weight nearly eight cwt. The hammer that strikes the hours is sixty pounds, and those that strike the quarters, twenty-six pounds. The chimes play every third hour, and perform the following tunes: Sicilian Mariners' Hymn, Abide with Me, and Keble's Evening Hymn.

Thanks to ALM for this extract from the Western Gazette and Flying Post Friday October 11, 1867. Ed

The Forlorn Hope: The Rossetti Family in Frome
by Keith Falconer

Photo: Keith Falconer

This is an account of how Frome interacted with the famous Rossetti family through a building, a painting at Longleat and a High-Church Anglican vicar. The title is taken from one of Christina's letters and reflects her perception of her move to Frome; the Forlorn Hope were the vanguard of an attack which had little hope of survival!

The Rossetti Family

Gabriele Pasquale Giuseppe Rossetti was born on 28 February 1783 in Vasto in the Kingdom of the Two Sicilies. Vasto was an ancient city with a somewhat turbulent history which, allied to a series of natural disasters, has destroyed most of its early buildings. In the 20th century it has grown into a settlement of some 40,000 population and shifted its focus to the marina and beaches but reveres the memory of Rossetti with its principal piazza named after him. Son of a blacksmith he was able to study at the University of Naples in 1804. In 1807 he was librettist at the San Carlo Opera House in Naples and was later appointed curator of ancient marbles and bronzes in the Capodimonte Museum in the city. His skill at improvising verses made him a society celebrity but his politically naive and impetuous nature was to get him into serious trouble.

Initially he had thrived under both the Bourbon and the Bonapartist regimes but had become a member of the revolutionary Carbonari Society and published patriotic poems and manifestos which, under the constitutional monarchy imposed on King Ferdinand in 1820 after his return, were well received. In 1831 his works on interpreting Dante led to his appointment as Professor of Italian at King's College, London, a post he held until 1847, by which time his sight was seriously impaired. When Rossetti became professor, he wrote propaganda calling for a liberally governed and united Italy and continued publishing his own poetry, his eccentric interpretation of Dante and his liberal treatises.

Rossetti's wife Frances Polidori, born in 1800, was the lynch pin of the family and her father, who lived to be ninety, was a very supportive grandparent. Though married to a lapsed Catholic, she was a staunch Anglican, as were her two daughters, and religion was to dominate the lives of all three Rossetti women.

When her husband's income was drying up in the 1840s due to ill health and failing eyesight, the family moved house in 1843 from Charlotte Street to Arlington Street, off Mornington Crescent in London where Frances was to open a day school assisted by Christina, as Maria had departed in 1844 to become a governess. The school was aimed at 'young ladies of good family' but seemed to have attracted only

Gabriele Rossetti by DG Rossetti the week before he came to Frome, 1853 Mrs Roderic O'Conor

daughters of local tradesmen and was never much of a success. It was Frances who organised the move to Frome in 1853 to open a day school but as her own mother was seriously ill, she was often away from Frome leaving Christina in charge of the house and school.

Frances Rossetti by DG Rossetti,1852 Birmingham Museum and Art Gallery

Her father, Gaetano Polidori was born in Tuscany in 1764, studied law at Pisa University and came to London in 1790 and married an English governess Anna Maria Pierce in 1793. He was a prolific writer and publisher and set up his own private press in his home in London where amongst other works he printed the first editions of some poems by his grandchildren Dante Gabriel and Christina. As a child Christina often stayed at his house in Holmer Green, Buckinghamshire and later he was much more a father figure to Christina than her own, rather infirm, father. His wife, however, who was a chronic invalid for her last twenty years never leaving her bedroom and was hardly an active influence on her grandchildren though her own family money was a regular support to Frances. One of their daughters, Charlotte Lydia, was to be a significant figure in the Rossetti family affairs.

Aunt Charlotte Lydia Polidori (1802-1890), called Aunt Incarnate by Dante, was governess and later companion to the Marchioness of Bath. She supported Dante and his work in numerous ways and in 1849 *The Girlhood of Mary, Virgin* was commissioned by the Marchioness of Bath for £80; it was his first sale. His mother and sister sat as models and it was the first painting to bear the initials PRB.* Aunt Charlotte also helped the rest of the Rossetti family throughout the 1840s, placing Maria as governess to the Thynne family and inviting Christina to holiday at Longleat where she was a welcome guest. Christina writes in January 1850 describing her stay in Longleat House 'in a large apartment containing two sofas and four arm chairs'. She has seen Dante's picture of the *Girlhood of Mary Virgin* in Lady Bath's sitting room but 'hung much too high', hence the Rossetti family were no strangers to Longleat and it was Aunt Charlotte who in 1853 prompted the Rossettis' move to Frome.

The Girlhood of Mary Virgin by DG Rossetti, 1849 Tate Gallery, London

In early 1850 Christina had to travel by rail to Bath or more likely Westbury Station which had opened in September 1848 and then by coach to Longleat, however when Christina returned to Longleat the following summer, the station at Frome, which was less than three miles away, had been open since October 1850 and when she returned home in August 1851, the French governess *charioteered* her to the station. Rev William Bennett had known the Rossettis in London. He was a prominent Anglo-Catholic and was Vicar of Frome Selwood from December 1851; he was responsible for the 'restoration' of St John's Church and the construction of the Via Crucis. He took a great interest in schools in Frome and was also responsible for the rebuilding of the Vicarage Street School. He remained in the town until his death on 17August 1886.

In the 1840s the Rossetti women, Frances, Maria and Christina, had come under the influence of the Anglo-Catholic movement in the Church of England led by Edward Pusey, a frequent preacher at the church in London where the Rossetti women worshipped. William Bennett's connection with the Rossetti family dates back to his incumbency as priest-in-charge of St Paul's Knightsbridge when he worked in the slums of Pimlico during the cholera outbreak in 1849 and had won the love and respect of his parishioners. When the new church of St Barnabas

*Pre-Raphaelite Brotherhood. Ed

44

opened in Pimlico the Puseyite nature of the sermons conducted there led to serious rioting and Bennett, at the request of his bishop, agreed to resign. Lady Bath offered him the living of Frome which was in her gift. Aunt Charlotte, Lady Bath's companion now suggested that a school at Frome, run under Bennett's auspices might prove more successful than the moribund school in Arlington Street.

After a happy family childhood and early family recognition of her prowess as a poet, Christina had just emerged from very troubled teenage girlhood years when she probably had a nervous breakdown and was still reeling from a broken engagement to James Collinson, one of the Pre-Raphaelite Brotherhood. With her mother and sister, Maria, she had become very involved in the high Anglican Church movement and had found solace by immersing herself in religion and was a cosmopolitan Londoner used to the cultural facilities of the capital.

Rev WJE Bennett by George Richmond Photo: Keith Falconer

She had sat as a model for two paintings by her brother Dante – the *Girlhood of Mary Virgin* and the *Annunciation* and for at least one by Collinson. Dante had also made a dozen sketches of his sister usually emphasising her studiousness; she was heavily involved in the affairs of the Pre-Raphaelite Brotherhood and with the publication of their literary magazine *The Germ.* Christina helped her mother with the school in Arlington Street since 1850 but in 1852 briefly visited Darlaston Hall in Staffordshire to tutor Swynfern Jervis's children in Italian. Swynfern Jervis MP was one of her father's literary friends.

The Move to Frome

Christina writes on the 30th March 1853 from Arlington Street; *Our London School having failed, Mamma has felt it her duty to avail herself of what appears to be a good opening for one at Frome in Somersetshire; so next Thursday (that is tomorrow week) we expect to leave town for that place. On the following Monday our school is to open; so you may imagine that we shall have plenty to do arranging our house during the few intervening days. Maria, Gabriel and William will continue here; - and Pappa also just for the present, though he is finally to join us, if the school answers.*

The move does not seem to have gone particularly well. Frances reported that they were dismayed to find the house with the painting and wall papering unfinished and a broken washstand completed the dismal picture. The building had clearly just been vacated by William Baxter, however Frances later writes that the arrival of the piano-forte and the family cat made it feel more like home and Dante's portrait of his father, produced on the 28th of April 1853 a week before he arrived in Frome, was proudly displayed over the mantelpiece in the drawing room. When on the 22nd of April Christina writes to her brother William she doesn't mention the move, the house itself or the school but says; *we have discovered some*

Christina Rossetti by DG Rossetti
Mrs Helen Rossetti Angeli

beautiful country hereabouts; abundance of green slopes and gentle declivities; no boldness or grandeur but plenty of peaceful beauty. ....pray thank Mr. Stephens; two of his figs are duly planted in our garden here against the warm wall.

It would appear that the Rossettis rented only one of the then two properties in the terrace and this almost certainly equates to 31 Fromefield but, as the other property was unoccupied, they had use of the whole garden. A few months later, in a letter to Amelia Heimann, her main pen-pal, Christina writes; *wish you could see our pretty little abode, with its really large drawing room, looking so cheerful now fires have commenced. The schoolroom, too, is quite comfortable, not feeling like a well when one enters it; and the other apartments are equally nice in their degree.*

Their settling in period, and the school routine, was to be severely interrupted. The following week Mrs Rossetti had to return to London where her mother was seriously ill and she arrived there just in time for her mother's death. Christina writes on the 28th of April; *Thank God indeed that dear Grandmamma died without pain and also that you left Frome when you did, another delay would have made you too late.*

Christina had to put the school affairs in order so that she herself could come 'up to town' involving a two week shortcoming. She also arranges that their housekeeper, a Mrs Bryant, would look after the house and have a daughter staying with her overnight, which Mr Bennett let her do at the vicarage.

Christina writes that; *If I come to London, and am in time, I should like to see Grandmamma again. Pray do not be afraid on the effects of such a sight on me; I really wish it unless the lapse of so many days renders it inadvisable.* Otherwise, she does not seem overly upset at her grandmother's death and is very matter of fact as to what mourning clothes she should pack for her mother and herself. She then devotes pages of the letter to detailed household matters including that; *This morning also arrived an official despatch from Heal & Sons announcing they had sent per rail the bed etc so these will probably come to hand today.* Obviously some personal furniture had yet to arrive.

Meanwhile her father, who was still in London writes unenthusiastically on 2nd May 1853 to an old Italian friend that he is about to go to Frome; *to leave there, these weary bones,* which was almost prophetic! In early May, Christina and her mother transferred father Rossetti to Frome with; *less inconvenience to Papa than we had anticipated. Now quite infirm he can only manage short walks around the garden which Christina remarks at last boasts of real gravel walks*.

Gabriele Rossetti was a spent force when he arrived in Frome with none of his former overwhelming exuberance. Christina laments; *Papa now hardly ever makes a remark or expresses opinion on public affairs. He occupies himself with letter writing to old friends in Italian and melancholy.* In July he writes; *My wife an excellent woman, has come here to set up a school for young ladies and I hope it will succeed.* He laments that, though William his son earns £300 a year and Maria £80 and Dante considerably more, times are hard. Besides regularly bemoaning the state of his health he discusses the latest Italian treatises including his own *Arpa Evangelica* which has just been published. This, he claims in a letter to his son Gabriel, has been well received in many states in Italy; *but in other parts the governments prohibit its entry, on account of the author's name, which has become a veritable scarecrow to Kings.* Indeed he advises his son, should he visit Italy, to use the name Dante Rossetti as the death sentence on Gabriele Rossetti had never been rescinded. In the same letter he adds a telling postscript; *I perceive that I have not spoken to you at all about the state of my health. And what can I say of it? It is the same as it was in London; betwixt life and death but more tending to the latter than the former.*

In December 1853 Grandfather Polidori was taken ill and Mrs Rossetti is again called up to London and on the 15th December her husband writes her a very pathetic letter lamenting her absence and begging for Polidori's comments on his *Arpa*. This crosses with a letter from his wife saying that her father was dying and indeed Polidori passed away the following day much to the distress of Christina and her father. Typically Rossetti claimed that; *I had deluded myself into supposing that my dear Polidori would shed tears for my death ... I shall soon join him and hope to embrace him again in the kingdom of happiness.* For once he was perhaps closer to the reality than he imagined.

The following week he pens another typically pathetic letter; *When are you going to return- when? Christina and I await you with open arms; but as yet in vain. Have you then decided to abandon Frome and to return to London? Hurrah!* He hopes that William is earning enough to unite the family under one roof – *as we do in Italy.* At the death of both the Polidori parents Mrs Rossetti inherited an income that, though small, was sufficient to make further school-teaching unnecessary and a return to London to unite the family was possible.

Life in Frome

Christina's letters from Frome give a flavour of the town at that time. Most of her letters are written to either Amelia Heimann, a close friend, or to William her brother.

The following extracts from Christina's letters may seem mostly domestic trivia, but they describe her activities beyond that of school teacher and nurse to her father and show that her sense of wit had not deserted her. Early on she writes; *I have discerned in Frome an Inn which I ought to patronize in preference to the George – the Blue Boar. Is it not a prevision of my sparkling self?* – This has been construed as a play on the word bore. Even while making arrangements to go up to London for her grandmother's funeral, and for appropriate mourning clothes, she reports on domestic affairs to her mother;

I hope to transact Aunt Charlotte's business, and to buy a suitable counterpane at Gilmore's. She then details paying for the windows to be cleaned; *Mr. Trotman's employees are cleaning the splashed outside of the window for 6d –well worth it, is it not? ..*she went to church at 3 o'clock, then paid for the chocolate pot which was; *simply a coffee pot with a mill and the cover made to admit its evolutions.* When living with William in London her father had been deprived of his coffee or chocolate and had to subsist on tea. She also paid a Mr Witcomb more than his estimate for re-upholstering the couch 'which has come home' with extra horsehair stuffing and trimmings.

In connection with her father's health she is concerned to have available medical help and she makes enquires of Amelia Heimann as to her mention of a Mr. Miller 'as a very able medical man' and as to where he lived. She had seen a notice to Slade & Miller (Surgeons) in the town – perhaps the same person? Later she hears of; *a Dr Harrison here, a very clever man we are told.* She notes; *There are sundry walks in our vicinity which we take at intervals sometimes discovering a new one to swell our stock. Pappa's walks are limited to our small garden: he is very feeble and we much wish to have our donkey and chaise but have not yet heard of anyone who will undertake to harbour them.* In October a little concerned about her mother's cold she observes; *....and of course one has to be extra watchful these days of cholera. When last this scourge was in England I hear that no, or at most one, case occurred at Frome.*

Her school activities are cause for concern; *Our school remains in status quo against this we may set the comfort of our scholars being nice, well-behaved children....If our school is meant to succeed, I should think very likely we might have an accession of pupils in July.* But in June she writes; *Our school re-opens on the 25th of next month whether with additional pupils I know not. We have been offered and have refused two boarders; in Pappa's state it would be impossible to have them as we are.* But also provide some enjoyment: *Last Monday we attended a feast given to some of the school children by Mr. Bennett. It was a hot afternoon and the sun baked one at the end of the room near the door... the room was made gay with flags, flowers, and inscriptions; and long lines of tables were laid out with cups, mugs etc. The viands were tea, perhaps coffee, bread and butter and cake. Mr. Bennett was there, looking as if he enjoyed the children's pleasure. He has a very benevolent expression.*

Somewhat later she writes; *Mamma and I attended the Midsummer examination of some of the Frome Church Schools. Mr. Bennett examined and distributed prizes. A few of the best boys and girls received really nice suits of clothes; not made in charity school fashion but of such materials and form as are now in vogue; the other rewards were small books etc. A small friend of mine obtained a prize, also the daughter of our laundress.*

She obviously misses the cosmopolitan facilities of the Capital and writes; *We shall probably subscribe to a book of books to be sent here quarterly from Mudie's in London and this may prove a resource to ourselves, and our friends as may favour us, as we hear there is not one good circulating library in Frome.* However somewhat later she reports that; *A society for having books down from London has just been formed and Mamma joined it. .... a book we must wish to get is Ruskin's new volume of The Stones of Venice.*

Whenever relatives come to stay it is cause for a family trip, she describes a typical outing; *While Willie was with us, Mamma treated herself, him and me, to an excursion to Wells. We had a nice little carriage, intended to hold two persons inside and one beside the driver on the box. But oh, the pouring rain that came on! Some time before reaching the destination, William took refuge with us inside; and the whole way home we were closely packed. However Wells Cathedral amply compensated for a little inconvenience. It is a fine gothic pile, not the finest I have seen, but possessed of its own individual merits. The drive was through a pretty country; partly through a rabbit-country, whose dusky inhabitants are allowed to live unmolested. Returning home we had a view of Nunney castle, a picturesque ivied ruin, quite to my taste.*

When her Aunt Eliza comes to stay she; ...*went with Mamma to Bath one day and brought me thence three genuine Bath buns, which bore a strong resemblance to their London namesakes.* And on another occasion; *Tomorrow, Maria and I plan devoting to an excursion to Bath. The Bath omnibus passes our garden gate, leaving Frome in the morning and returning in the evening. The fare is 2s 6d a head each way; and one remains about six hours in Bath, which gives ample time for exploration.* After several vain attempts to attain and house a donkey and chaise she thinks that; *perhaps a Bath chair which can be hired here for a shilling an hour will answer quite as well for pappa if he likes to make use of one, and be less troublesome and even less expensive.* It is on her sister Maria's departure that she then comes up with my title; *she leaves us on that day to our sorrow; though I am heartily content that she still lives in London instead of having to swell the Frome forlorn hope!*

Family and daily trivia, and indeed local gossip, fill these letters including; ... *a short time ago our landlord sent us a liberal present of gooseberries and black currants; the latter have been made into jam and now present a goodly array of thirteen jars ...duly protected with paper dipped in brandy and surmounted by bladder... On Saturday Mamma and Maria called on Mr Bennett. Lord Charles Thynne, with whom Maria used to be, is coming to Frome. He is in quite reduced circumstances and has undertaken the very inferior office of Sacristan.*

The surviving correspondence tails off in November and December but we know that Christina wrote to her grandfather soliciting comments on a poem and that she was devastated by his death - breaking down completely weeping and crying and caused a hiatus in her correspondence prolonged by her own father's deterioration in health in January. When the letters resume in February we learn that Maria, Gabriel and William had paid a flying visit prompted by a further deterioration in their own father's health and comforted themselves; *with the hope of a not far distant meeting at home again.* Indeed they obviously discussed where a suitable house might be found in London and by the end of the month they may have been fixing upon a house in Upper Albany Street, Regents Park. They still had time for long walks relishing; *the sight of early wild flowers blowing and delightful lambs with their comfortable mothers.* One puzzling reference in her letter of 23rd February is that; *Tomorrow (which was a Friday) being fair day we are to be blockaded in our house by horned beasts: they are not my forte.*

Only one further letter, on the 27th March 1854 is addressed from Fromefield and the next is in May from 45 Upper Albany Street in London. The family's exile in Frome was over but, as Berta Lawrence was to put it; *out of that dreary year blossomed a number of Christina's poems, several of them very beautiful!* She wrote over a score of poems including Sleep at Sea, Holy Innocents, Annie, Seasons, Whitsun Eve, Two Parted and the Bourne. She also wrote a ditty as an Epitaph to the Pre-Raphaelite Brotherhood and *Charon* which begins *In my Cottage near the Styx* an allusion, according to William, to Brunswick Place.

Rossetti Epilogue

In April 1854 the Rossetti Family rented a house in Albany Street and on the 26th Gabriele, the father, died there. He was buried in May 1854 in Highgate Cemetery which, opened in 1839, had already attracted an illustrious clientele. Despite protestations from the Italian exile community for a high profile ceremony for their erstwhile idol, his wife Frances, who had purchased the grave slot, insisted on a quiet family affair and a rather modest tombstone. The grave with two more inscribed stones, was to be the resting place of all the family and their immediate descendants except for Dante. A few months after her father's death Christina volunteered to go with Florence Nightingale to nurse in the Crimea but much to her distress she was turned down as too young and inexperienced, while her Aunt Eliza Polidori was accepted. I have found no evidence that Christina ever returned to Frome and that unfortunate episode in the family's life seems to have been quickly forgotten within the family but is always mentioned by biographers as a significant element in the family's dynamics.

1 The Letters of Christina Rossetti, Volume 1, edited by Anthony H Harrison, The University Press of Virginia, 1997

S O M E R S E T S H I R E

TO be LETT, and entered upon at Michaelmas next, at Frome Selwood;
All that commodious INN, called the ANCHOR, adjoining the Wool-hall and Shambles, now in the occupation of Mr John Lambert, under-tenant to Mrs Rogers; consisting of a large dining-room and convenient and lofty chambers, cellars, a wine-vault, 4 stables, a large yard with a thorough-fare to the market, being the second best and largest inn in Frome. Also a spacious and commodious Messuage adjoining, having a good parlour with marble chimney-piece, a dressing-room, large kitchen with stew-holes, brew-house, furnace & boiler, good stable for 3 or 4 horses, a large hay-loft that extends to the Anchor barton, and a passage thro' the same and the front to the church steps; lately inhabited by Mr George Whitchurch, attorney: It is fit for a gentleman and lady out of trade, or may be fitted up for a clothier. --- Good tenants may depend upon encouragement. For further particulars, apply to Mr Edward Newport, or Mr Richard Watts, clothier, in Frome; or Samuel Allen, King's-square, Bristol.
Thanks to ALM for this advertisement from The Bath Chronicle 21.X.1784. Ed

Edward Flatman was born at Market Weston, Suffolk, the son of a miller and innkeeper. He bought Keyford College in 1848 when there were six resident students but he developed the school giving a solid education to the students. He was one of the first members of the Frome Local Board and was the Chairman for 10 years as well as serving on many committees including Frome Gas Works, Frome-Selwood Permanent Building Society, the Board of Guardians and he was Treasurer of the Dissenters Cemetery.

During his chairmanship, Frome obtained the Town Water Works and Sewerage Scheme, Infectious Hospital and Recreation Ground. He was an Alderman and County Councillor and gave the clock on the public offices (now the Town Hall) on Christchurch Street West which bears his name.

He died on 1st January 1894; amongst many tributes to him, Samuel Rawlings said that he was a man whose sympathies were with the poor, who, with his death, had lost a very true friend.

Warfare in the West Country
by Hilary Daniel

We in the West Country live in a part of England which has for the most part escaped the worst experiences of warfare. Apart from three or four comparatively short periods of fairly intensive fighting, most of the past two thousand years have seen the belligerent kings and barons passing us by as they hasten on to their great battles elsewhere.

The Romans, for instance, when they began to occupy Britain under Claudius in 43 AD, did most of their decisive fighting against the British tribes in the Home Counties, East Anglia, Wales and the Scottish frontier, and the only connection that we West countrymen have with the rebellion of the fierce Boadicea - "the British warrior queen, bleeding from the Roman rods" who "sought with an indignant mien counsel from her nation's gods"[1] - was that the fiery statue of her on Westminster Bridge was cast a century ago in the works of J W Singer at Frome. After that our local tribe, the Belgae, gave the Romans little trouble, and they settled down among us, built their villas and farms, such as that at Whatley, laid out strategic roads such as the Fosseway, and intermarried with the regional chieftains' families. Together we all enjoyed four hundred years of fairly peaceful prosperity.

Boadicea on Westminster Bridge

When the Franks and Germans attacked the Roman frontier on the Rhine, the Emperors could no longer afford the men and materials to maintain forces in our isolated provinces, and the legions were withdrawn in 425 AD, but although the invading Jutes, Angles and Saxons, starting with Hengist and Horsa, shortly afterwards began to conquer and settle the South East of Britain, our own part of the country held out for another two hundred and fifty years, and local chiefs and kinglets endeavoured to preserve the Romano-British way of life.

During this obscure period one name emerges from what are generally known as the Dark Ages, that of Arthur. Although many mythical legends have grown up around him, most historians now concede that he quite probably did exist, and that he is most likely to have been a West Country chieftain from one of those Romano-British families who still ruled their principalities as far as possible on Roman lines. His achievement seems to have inspired the Britons to resist the spread of the Anglo-Saxons, and in a decisive battle at Mount Badon in about 500 AD he scored such a victory that he dissuaded the Saxons from advancing further into the South-West for nearly two hundred years.

There are several theories as to where Mount Badon was, but there is a good case for identifying it with Badbury near the great earthwork of Liddington Castle a few miles South-East of Swindon. Other suggestions have been the other Badbury, at Badbury Rings in Dorset, or a hill near Bath, but the Wiltshire location seems to be the most likely. The battle was first engaged down below the Castle, but according to the ancient chronicler Geoffrey of Monmouth, Arthur's men pressed hard on the Saxons, who were drawn up on higher ground in a number of wedge formations, and the latter were forced to retreat into the hilltop fortress for the night. In the morning Arthur renewed his attack, and Geoffrey records that his men struggled up the slope of the 300ft hill, being met by furious assaults of Saxon detachments charging down with the force of gravity on their side. However, with enormous courage the Britons fought their way to the top, and the Saxons took to their heels and retreated to their more settled lands in the Thames Valley.

The Ridgeway near Liddington

Fifty years later the Saxons were on the move again. Their king Cynric captured Old Sarum (Salisbury) in 552, and by 556 Cynric and his son Cealwin had reached the Swindon area again. Twenty years later they had a very important strategic goal in mind. Three little kingdoms were clustered in South Gloucestershire and North Somerset, with their capitals at Gloucester, Bath and Cirencester. Cealwin realised that this disunity gave him the opportunity to push through their poorly defended territories to reach the Severn Estuary, and although the three kings gathered their armies together to try to bar his way, he surrounded them, killed all three of them, and put their armies to flight.

This battle took place near Dyrham House in 577, close to where the M4 now crosses the A46 near Old Sodbury, and was probably one of the most significant in the early history of our islands. The Battle of Dyrham effectively split the British lands into two, and the Northern Britons were forced to retreat into Wales, where their descendants still live and talk their ancient language, while the Southern Celts, cut off from their Welsh relatives, were gradually forced down into Cornwall, and numbers of them eventually crossed the Channel to Brittany, where they still keep up the ancient Cornish ways under the French flag.

But after Dyrham the invading Saxons turned North into the Midlands, where they founded the new kingdom of Mercia, which soon became the most powerful of the

Heptarchy of seven states that made up the government of what was gradually turning into the English nation. Our Western lands were not at that time very attractive for settlement. The Saxons had already occupied Salisbury Plain, but running West from Warminster and Trowbridge was the thick damp sallow forest of Selwood, and beyond that again were the impenetrable marshes of the Somerset Levels, and yet further on the barren wastes of Exmoor and Dartmoor. Clearly nobody was going to be particularly interested in carving a living out of those sorts of terrains, so the West Country was left strictly alone for over a century. It was not until 685 that the Saxons thrashed the South Britons at Penselwood, a couple of miles from Stourhead, and moved in to start clearing settlements such as Frome and Bruton out of the Forest.

But these pioneers were a hardy lot, and their little realm of Wessex, the kingdom of the West Saxons, was soon expanding and becoming a state to be reckoned with. With its capital at Winchester it was well placed to dominate the South coast as far as Sussex and Kent, and just like the United States in the 19th Century it had its wild Western frontier lands in Somerset, Dorset and Devon, where an enterprising individual who was quick on the draw could make his fortune very quickly.

But it was the Midland state of Mercia that was the dominant power in the 8th Century, and the ferocious King Offa, who reigned from 758 to 796, was the first really great ruler whom these islands have produced. In 777 he temporarily quashed the pretensions of the infant state of Wessex by beating King Kenulf at a battle near Wallingford; he then turned his attention to his Welsh neighbours, constructing the great defensive earthwork that still bears his name, Offa's Dyke. Kenulf, still licking his wounds after his defeat, looked on these proceedings with interest, and, concluding that sauce for the gander would also suit the goose, he seems to have decided that a good defensive dyke would be a useful thing to protect Wessex against any further invasions by Offa. So within a few years he too was building his own great earthwork to defend his Northern frontier against Mercia, stretching from the Bristol Channel past Bath into Berkshire, and even today as you drive North out of Devizes you can still see the Wansdyke prominently snaking its way across the Marlborough Downs.

By the 820s the King of Mercia was an ambitious soldier Beornwulf, whose covetous eyes were directed towards the conquest of Wessex. King Egbert of Wessex, however, perhaps confident behind his rampart of Wansdyke, was continuing to bring pressure to bear on the unfortunate Britons down in Cornwall. But by 825 Egbert was sufficiently concerned about the Mercian threat to bring his army North to confront Beornwulf's men near Swindon. Here at Ellandun, thought to be in the area of Wroughton, he attacked the Mercians on an oppressively hot day, and after a long struggle against vastly superior numbers he broke their ranks and King Beornwulf, in the curious words of the chronicler "sought for flight and would not have lost his spurs for three halfpence". With that one battle the power of Mercia was broken for good, and we of Wessex took our rightful place as the leaders of the English nation - without Egbert's great victory think of the state that the country would now be in.

But now a new threat was already building up all round our shores. In 789 three Viking ships put in near Weymouth and the crews, apparently without provocation, murdered the Reeve of Dorchester who had come down to see what was happening. Soon the Northmen were turning up all round the coast, and were raiding any settlement within a reasonable distance of the sea.

Then in 865 the Danes invaded with what was called the Great Army, and within a few years their leaders, the brothers Halfdan and Ingwaer, had occupied huge swathes of Northern and Eastern England, an area that became known as the Danelaw, and were bringing over their families with a view to establishing permanent settlements. Ingwaer, in particular, spread terror wherever he went: a chronicler records "And the aforesaid Ingwaer stalked through the land like a wolf, and slaughtered the people, man, woman and the unwitting child, and drove to misery the defenceless Christians". And it was regarded fully as a religious war; the writers of the Anglo-Saxon Chronicle frequently refer to the Vikings as "heathens" and to the Saxons as "Christians".

A coalition of the Heptarchy, led by Ethelred I (not the Unready) managed to defeat the Great Army at Ashdown near Reading in 871, but this did not remove the threat. Three months later Ethelred's younger brother Alfred succeeded him, and the early years of his reign marked a continuous process of retreat in the face of ever-increasing Danish pressure.

One of the Danish leaders, Guthrum, captured Exeter in 875 after a spectacular advance and a certain amount of trickery, but his fleet was scattered by a storm. Then, early in 878, Guthrum surprised Alfred at Chippenham, where he had been celebrating Christmas, and by Easter Alfred had been driven back into the mid-Somerset marshes at Athelney; from the A361 near The Mump at Boroughbridge you can see the monument which marks his presence there among the marshes and meres of the Somerset Levels, and the place where he is alleged to have burnt the cakes.

Regrettably we have to dismiss that story about Alfred burning the cakes as a bit of romantic fiction. There is no evidence that his stay at Athelney was as a fugitive in disguise, and it is clear that in fact he spent those spring months being very busy in a proper royal and military way. He certainly had some forces at his command, and one detachment of these managed to beat off a Danish landing near Countisbury Hill. What he did succeed in doing was to keep in close touch with all his scattered men, to gather them together, and to drill them into a small but very capable army. He ensured that the fyrds, the territorial forces of the counties of Somerset, Dorset and Wilts, and of West Hants, were got ready, and as soon as he felt himself strong enough he sent despatches summoning them to join him where three counties meet, near where Alfred's Tower now stands above Stourhead. From there he marched Northeast to intercept Guthrum, who was coming South from Chippenham with his troops, and at the edge of Salisbury Plain, somewhere near the villages of Edington and Bratton, the two armies met. After a bitter struggle Guthrum was roundly defeated and sued for peace. The peace treaty was signed at Wedmore, close to Alfred's headquarters at Athelney, and Guthrum and his army were compulsorily converted to Christianity (Guthrum and thirty of his chief officers being baptised at Aller near Langport, with Alfred as Guthrum's godfather). Guthrum himself retired into East Anglia, where he made himself king in 880, and agreed with Alfred on their mutual boundary. Tradition says that the Westbury White Horse, the symbol of Wessex cut into the chalk, was made to commemorate the victory. By 886 Alfred was recognised as King of all the Saxons in the South and West, while the Danelaw continued to comprise the North and East.

As a result of this Battle of Edington, Wessex enjoyed a period of comparative peace and prosperity, though some minor battles with the Danes were inevitable; they made incursions towards Wiltshire and Gloucester in support of Ethelwold, Alfred's nephew, who disputed the succession of Edward the Elder after Alfred's death. A fleet of Danes attacked Watchet in 914, and, being driven off, landed on the islands of Flatholm and Steepholm in the Bristol Channel to recover. The English kept a close watch on them and set up a blockade, and in the autumn they were eventually starved out. Alfred encouraged learning and the rule of law, and as founder of our navy he showed his belief in safety through strength. Some of his successors, however, were made of weaker stuff, and it was Ethelred II who earned the nickname of Unready, used in its old sense of having no clear policies and being unwilling to accept advice. He it was who ordered in 1002 a massacre of all the Danes in his kingdom, and when this inevitably led to fierce reprisals he pursued a policy of paying the invaders to go away, imposing a tax called Danegeld to raise the necessary money; the Danes, of course, accepted it with both hands, departed, and faithfully came back year after year for more.

Within a few years, however, the Northmen made another attempt at permanent conquest, and Ethelred fled to the Continent, leaving his successor Edmund, nick-named Ironside, to defend a weakened kingdom. In a lightning campaign in 1016, by a series of six brilliant engagements, starting here with another Battle of Penselwood, Edmund drove the Danes back right across the country to Essex. Sadly, though, there he met his match when he faced the Danish leader Canute at Assingdon on 18 October. His trusted theign, Edric Streona, turned traitor in the midst of the battle and held back his right wing, so that Canute's left was able to outflank the unlucky Edmund. Thus Edmund Ironside, the last great Anglo-Saxon hero, died heartbroken six weeks later, and Canute was crowned King of England and soon afterwards King of Denmark too.

That second Battle of Penselwood was the last significant engagement on West Country soil for many centuries. We were not involved in the struggle of the Norman Conquest, and were only on the edge of the chaotic civil war between King Stephen and his cousin the Empress Matilda, and the later conflict between King John and his barons. The Hundred Years War passed us by, though doubtless West Country men fought at Crecy in 1346, and they definitely did at Agincourt in 1415, for there is a memorial window in Gloucester Cathedral to the dead of that battle. The Wars of the Roses, too, were fought out in other parts of the country, the nearest battle being the final defeat of the Lancastrians in 1471 at Tewkesbury, which is virtually in the

Midlands. Western seamen were prominent in Queen Elizabeth's navy during the life-and-death war with Spain, but the only time that hostilities touched us directly was when in 1588 Sir Francis Drake and others followed the Armada from Plymouth up the English Channel to its complete destruction by battle and storm.

But then in 1625 King Charles I came to the throne, aged 25. Inflexibly convinced that he had been specially chosen by God to rule, and that he had what he called the Divine Right of Kings to rule as he thought fit, he soon began to stir up very considerable opposition. Problems arose over the deep unpopularity of some of his ministers, over the Puritan distrust of Charles' High Church tendencies, and especially over his insistence on imposing taxes without the consent of Parliament. In 1642 Civil War broke out between the Royalist and the Parliamentary factions.

The Civil War is a very difficult one to describe or to follow. There was no clear North/South division as in the American Civil War, nor East/West as in Spain in the 1930s; support for Cavaliers or Roundheads split counties, towns and even families into a veritable jigsaw which is quite bewildering when shown on a map. Individual towns or even single castles or mansions would hold out, sometimes for years, in the middle of great swathes of hostile territory. Taunton, for instance, supported Parliament, and was besieged by the Royalists for a couple of years, while Sherborne Castle was held for the King amidst surrounding Roundheads for a period at the beginning of the War. The King held Oxford and the South Midlands as his main base, while Parliament kept London, the Home Counties and East Anglia. The rest of the country was an enormous chessboard round which the rival armies chased one another trying to achieve tactical advantage at any opportunity.

Although hostilities had broken out in the summer of 1642, it was not until October that the first real battle took place, at Edgehill near Banbury, which both sides claimed as a victory, but at which the King probably took a slight advantage.

Meanwhile there was a considerable amount of activity in our own part of the country, where the King's Lieutenant of the Horse in the West, Sir Ralph Hopton, Squire of Witham Friary near Frome, was busy clearing up pockets of anti-Royalist disaffection in Devonshire. In the course of this he came into contact with a doughty Cornish worthy, Sir Bevil Grenville, with whose support he defeated the last Western Parliamentarian force at Stratton, near Bude, on 16th May, when Grenville's foot soldiers successfully charged the Roundhead army defending an almost unassailable position at the top of a steep hill.

Sir Bevil Grenville was the grandson of Sir Richard Grenville the Elizabethan sailor, whose action in pitting the "Revenge" against a whole Spanish fleet had been so legendary. He himself was also of a courageous nature, and having been converted to the Royalist cause he put his whole strength into supporting it. He raised five regiments of infantry and one of cavalry, and when Hopton set out from Cornwall in an attempt to join the King in an attack on the strategic centre of Bristol, Grenville's men formed a vital part of his force. Leaving Devon behind, Hopton's army advanced though Chard, Glastonbury and Wells, and so up onto the Mendips. At Chewton Mendip on a misty June evening they encountered their first Roundheads and put them to flight, and then continued on through Frome and Bradford-on-Avon towards Bath, where they intended to cut the Parliamentary communications between Bristol and London.

Circling round to the East of Bath, Hopton made for Lansdown Hill, which dominates the city, and found it occupied by his old friend Sir William Waller, now on the opposing side, with a strong force of men and guns. Hoping to take Waller in the rear, Hopton pressed up to Cold Ashton and Freezing Hill, and next morning moved round to attack. He found Waller's men and their cannons lined up along the Northern edge of Lansdown Hill on either side of the steep road leading down in the direction of Wick, along a stone wall which gave them some shelter.

As they had done at Stratton, the Cornish infantry, supported by cavalry, charged up the steep slope into the muzzles of the enemy guns. This was in practice not quite so dangerous as it might seem, since the slope was so acute that the guns could not be used at close quarters, because if depressed below the horizontal to aim directly at the enemy, the cannon balls would roll out before they could be fired. Musket fire, however, was quite another thing, and the defenders caused many casualties among those charging up the slope. Five times the Roundhead horsemen counter-charged down among the struggling attackers, five times they were dispersed, and eventually the Cornishmen breasted the defenders' wall; the latter withdrew to another part of the hilltop. But in the moment of victory the Cornishmen suffered a terrible loss, as Sir Bevil himself was poleaxed and slain on the brow of the hill, where his fine memorial still stands today.

Sir Bevil Grenville's monument

Night was now coming on and hostilities were broken off by mutual consent. The next morning Hopton found that during the night Waller had evacuated the hill and marched his army away. But yet another blow was to strike the Royalists; as Hopton moved among the wounded an ammunition wagon blew up, blinding and paralysing him. With their commander out of action the Cavaliers abandoned their advance on Bristol, and set off through Marshfield towards the East, sending Prince Maurice ahead to ask for reinforcements from the King in Oxford. This was doubly necessary because during the fierce fighting at Lansdown a number of horsemen had prematurely decided that the field was lost and had galloped off to bring the King inaccurate tidings of a defeat.

In due course they reached Devizes, where it was decided that Hopton was so ill that they had better stay there until the reinforcements arrived, but it was soon found that this had been a mistake. Waller, learning of the Royalists' plight, had reversed his original intention of retreating and had harried the Royalist rear. He now occupied Roundway Down, a bare hill to the North, from which he began to bombard the town. He later came down to lay on a siege. Hopton, blind and paralysed, was still able to exercise command, and did what he could to bring his dispirited men back into fighting condition. It is said that there was a severe shortage of match for firing the guns, and that the inhabitants of Devizes had all their bedcords confiscated to be cut into suitable lengths; the whole situation was grim.

But now, as so often happened in that strange war, the tables were suddenly turned once more. Prince Maurice, having made incredible time in his mission to Oxford and back, accompanied by a strong force of cavalry, took Waller by complete surprise and occupied Roundway Hill behind him. Waller sent his own horsemen up to try and dislodge the Prince, but they were driven down again in disarray, and galloped back through the ranks of their own infantry, causing great confusion. By this time the gallant Hopton was also issuing out of Devizes to attack, and the whole Roundhead army was put to ignominious flight.

The way was now open for Hopton, who was by that time beginning to recover his sight and the use of his limbs, to resume his advance on Bristol through Bath, while at the same time Prince Rupert was leading another force to Bristol through Chipping Sodbury. After intense street fighting the city fell, and the focus of the War moved to other parts of the country. The next year, 1643, some minor clearing up sorties were mounted by the Royalists at Exeter and Torrington, but the West did not feature in operations until the last few months of hostilities, by which time the Parliamentarians had finally attained the ascendancy.

Fairfax and Cromwell then came in pursuit of the Royalist general, Goring, who was trying to finish off the siege of Taunton. On 10 July 1645 Fairfax caught up with Goring at the ford, now a bridge, a mile or so East of Langport on the Somerton road. The Roundhead horse charged twice into the narrow valley, and when a third and reinforced attack became imminent the Cavaliers fled and Goring's army disintegrated. Fairfax amused himself by knocking off various small castles still held

Nunney Castle

for the King, such as Nunney and Farleigh Hungerford, which were both "slighted" (i.e. had their fortifications demolished), and in the autumn he, with Waller and Cromwell, slowly forced the Prince of Wales, later Charles II, to escape through Devon and Cornwall and off via the Scilly Isles.

So ended the West's participation in a war that would lead, in time, to the execution of the King in 1649, and to England's unsuccessful experiment with establishing a Republic. Only the genius of the Commonwealth Admiral Blake, who was a native of Bridgwater, where his fine statue stands, and who distinguished himself in the Dutch wars, connects us with those times, which ended with the restoration of the monarchy under Charles II in 1660.

Charles II, the Merry Monarch, having kept the peace and fathered many children during his twenty-five years' reign, died in 1685, leaving the throne to his Catholic brother James II. James, as Duke of York, had been an excellent High Admiral, but he was a disaster as a King, having inherited all his father's stubbornness and short-sightedness as to the inevitable consequences of his actions. Many of his new Protestant subjects were genuinely afraid that the accession of a Catholic to the throne would lead to a return to the intolerance and burnings at the stake of the time of Queen Mary, and when one of Charles II's illegitimate sons, the Duke of Monmouth, a popular and successful soldier, landed at Lyme with a story that his mother had after all been legally married to his royal father, he found many country folk willing to listen to this Protestant's claim to the throne. Marching up to Taunton, he was there proclaimed King, and leading a rather motley band of followers, some armed only with scythes and pitchforks, he set off towards Bristol and Bath. Meeting strong opposition, lacking any clear plan, and realising that he was not going to be able to raise much further support, he turned round and retreated through Norton St. Philip, where there was a short skirmish. Monmouth nearly lost his life to a bullet fired at him through a window of the George Inn, and eventually got back to Bridgwater, where he heard that King James' army was close behind him and encamped on Sedgemoor. Knowing that his untrained followers would be no match for his professional pursuers, he decided that a surprise attack would be his only hope. Marching stealthily out from Bridgwater by night, he approached the loyalist camp near Westonzoyland, but his undisciplined men encountered an unexpected ditch full of water, the Bussex Rhine, and in trying to cross it they made so much noise that the alarm was given and the King's army turned on them, causing them to flee in total disorder. Many of them were slaughtered by the troops of Colonel Kirk, Africa-hardened by service in Tangier, "Kirk's Lambs" as he facetiously called them. Monmouth himself was executed without trial, and King James sent the infamous Judge Jefferies down to conduct the Bloody Assizes, where he sentenced hundreds of simple countrymen to be hanged or transported overseas.

But Britain had soon had enough of James. Not only was the vicious persecution of the West Country held against him, but he did many things that were politically inept. He had only two children, both by a previous marriage, Princess Mary and Princess Anne, who were staunch Protestants, and many English people would have been prepared to keep their heads down and wait for time to relieve them of their unsuitable King. However, in the midst of all these crises, James II new Catholic queen produced a son.

The thought of yet another Catholic succession was the last straw, and an invitation went out to Princess Mary and her husband, William of Orange, the ruler of Holland, to come over and set things right.

The George Inn, Norton St Philip

William duly arrived, backed by a considerable Dutch fleet, at Brixham, and began to travel slowly up the country towards London. James brought his army part way to intercept him, but on Salisbury Plain many of his officers began to desert, and James, seeing that the situation was hopeless, returned to London and eventually he, his wife and his baby son fled the country. William halted at the Bear Inn at Hungerford and there negotiated terms with delegates from Parliament, and when all was settled, he entered the capital and he and his wife were proclaimed joint sovereigns.

The whole "Glorious Revolution", as it was called, had taken place with scarce a shot being fired, and our Western Counties had played a prominent part in yet another momentous event in our nation's history.

From that time on our land has been blessedly free of invasion or civil war. West Country people have, of course, played their full part in the Napoleonic, Crimean and Boer Wars and in the great World conflicts of 1914 and 1939. In the last of those our Western towns and cities suffered greatly from bombing, and our airfields, naval stations and army camps were used to great effect. In Korea the Glorious Gloucesters won themselves undying fame, but these conflicts are all so fully and expertly documented elsewhere that it would be unnecessary, and indeed impossible, to deal with them in this short essay.

[1] *Boadicea, an Ode by William Cowper*

St John's College in Wallbridge House, Frome

62

The Diary and Memoirs of John Allen Giles Part III

At the end of the year 1823 it was thought by all my friends that Frome Grammar School was not exactly the place where I could obtain the necessary final tuition for entering the University of Oxford, but another half year was allowed to slip away before anything decisive was done. The Charterhouse at this time enjoyed a well-earned reputation under its Head Master Dr Russell, and it was determined that I should go there at the beginning of the next term. In the month of June therefore, the very time of the year when at my former schools I should have been looking forward to six weeks of holidays, I bade adieu to my school-fellows, leaving my brother William, with my cousin Douglas Giles, after their usual vacation, to resume their studies under Mr Williams as before. It was, I believe, on the first day of June that I first went to London by the Frome coach in company with my father and another friend who was going there on business of his own. The cloak which my father wore on this journey, and which had been made for him in the preceding winter, is hanging up in Churchill Court, fifty years since it was made.

After thirteen hours spent on our journey we reached London and put up at the Castle and Falcon an inn that was then thought highly respectable, and it may still be for aught I know to the contrary, in Aldersgate Street. As everything was novel to me, it has not escaped my memory that we had lobsters and cold meat for supper. The next morning we set out after breakfast to perambulate London and see whatever might be worth seeing in that, to me unknown, metropolis. For this purpose we had come up two or three days before the school opened, but I have not the slightest recollection of any thing that I saw during those days, nor can I boast of the same power of observation which my father possessed. He never came home without some anecdote of what he had seen. On his way home after leaving me at the Charterhouse, whilst sitting on the box of the Frome coach at the White Horse Cellar in Piccadilly, he saw a man staggering by under a heavy load of bacon. One of the ostlers who were attending on the horses went behind him and with a large clasp knife cut off a huge piece of the bacon, and began to eat it on the spot. The man who carried the bacon did not notice the diminution of load, and went on as if nothing had happened.

Sometimes the power of observation was directed towards politics in which he always took great interest, and on one occasion he exercised great foresight, but whether before the year 1824 or after, I am not able to say. He told us, on coming home one evening from London, that he had entered the shop of a tailor somewhere in London, when the master of the shop said "There's Lord Palmerston; I wonder why he is coming back so soon: he goes by here to and fro every day." My father knew that there was a talk of Parliament breaking up, and he knew that at this time many of its members, including his lordship, were much in debt and could be arrested, when no longer protected by their privilege of parliament. Putting these facts together he reported in the country that a dissolution or prorogation of parliament was imminent; and the next day his prediction was fulfilled.

Not a particle of this power of observation has descended to me. My chief attention was given to the book-sellers' shops which we saw as we passed through the streets. I have always shown a love of books, even for their own sake generally, without much appreciation of their contents. I once got possession of a small book in German, and although I could not read a word of it, nor knew even what it was about, I spent 2 shillings in having it bound that I might have the pleasure of seeing it on the shelf alongside of my other books about which I did know something. My father was angry, said "A fool and his money are soon parted," and threw my unlucky book into the fire. Of this hasty act he repented before he went to bed, and the next day he brought me the beautiful edition of Young's Night Thoughts illustrated by Westall, to supply the place of the trumpery book which he had burnt. In London I could hardly escape doing something in the book line. I bought a bad edition of Butler's Hudibras, and found it utterly impossible for me to understand, and so went the first half crown of the many thousands which I have since spent in buying books and in exchanging one edition for another. He who wishes to form a good library should study Bibliography, or take the advice of someone who has done so, and make up his mind clearly as to the class of books that he wants his library to consist of.

On the 4th of June my father went with me to the Charterhouse. We were shown into the drawing-room of Mr Watkinson the second master; and after a few minutes the reverend gentleman himself appeared, and I think he never occupied so high a place in my admiration as during the first half-hour that I spent in his company and in his house. During the few minutes that preceded his entrance I had time to notice the extensive and respectable library that filled the room, for being an old bachelor he made the same room his drawing room and his book- room, and I should like to have asked him why he arranged the volumes of the same work from right to left, instead of from left to right, as they are generally arranged in book-cases: but my awe of him prevented my mounting to such a height of familiarity.

I was now however occupied in looking over my papers of different kinds, and found some original letters, one of which was written by Sir Walter Scott to Mr Jeanes Mrs Williams's father, and I copied it into my Manuscript volume of Miscellanies. The annexed letter to Arthur, about this time, arrived from his cousin John L. Dalley, whose family were now living at Newry, where his father was Collector of the Customs.

My dear little Arthur.-

I hope the contents of this little box will amuse you and your dear little sister Izzy. You must write me a long letter when you are big enough to go to school and wear a jacket and trous... inexpressibles. I hope you will not pull the tails off the horses, or the noses off the drivers.

Your affectionate
Cousin. JOHN

Whether the singular anecdote of Cardini belongs to this date or twenty years later, I cannot tell. My scraps have often been thrown together without distinction and been disinterred after a very long time. Witness the sketches which Thackeray made in my drawing room at Bridgewater about the year 1832, and brought to light in 1864.

The extremes of high and low spirits, which occur in the same person at different times, are happily illustrated by the following case. A physician in one of the cities of Italy was once consulted by a gentleman, who was much distressed by a paroxysm of this intermitting state of hypochondriasm. He advised him to seek relief in convivial company, and advised him in particular to find out a gentleman of the name of Cardini, who kept all the tables in the city, to which he was occasionally invited, in a roar of laughter. "Alas! sir," said the patient, with a heavy sigh, "I am that Cardini." Many such characters, alternately marked by high and low spirits, are to be found in all the cities of the world.

Wednesday, March 9. A great panic in London on money matters. The Rev Matthew Anderson, minister of East Dulwich chapel, writes thus in a letter addressed to me about Venerable Bede's works: "Some of our wealthy friends and neighbours would support the work; but the times are bad. Mr Hichens who might have been of great service in ordinary times, is so shaken with these Exchequer bills, (of which he holds £52,500) that he is unable to move in anything. I am sorry I cannot let you have my copy of the book you name, to print from; but I value it too highly for its very curious binding. I would still waive this objection if it were a rare book, and would readily offer him on the altar of patriotism and venerability; but the book is common enough."

Grimsthorpe, Bourn, March 14

Dear Allen

Put down my name on your list, and I will try to get you another subscriber. Whether 1 can ever pay my subscription is very questionable. I can hardly tell how badly off I am, with a very distant chance of improvement. My brother Henry seems likely to do pretty well; and Edward of course is all right, but the others of my family are very near to extinction, and will be no better off until the death of our old grandmother. My mother's income is only £130 a year, with five girls and Robert to dispose of; and I have an income of £150 a year with a charge of £25 for interest and insurance. So, although you have had such heavy blows dealt you lately, you are not the only one who is wretched. I think some αλαϲτωρ, as Aeschylus would have said, has "leapt a leap" upon our family roof. But have we not both deserved our calamities. My mother had a frightful epileptic attack early on Sunday morning, and I feared for some minutes her reason was gone. She is wonderfully better today. What a pity it is Mrs James Toogood is so tormented with the cacoethes scribendi. She is no fool, but not up to authorship. Mr Jeanes's house, now the property of the Williamses (S Bundy Williams and wife) is one of the best in Charmouth. I only doubt whether it will sell at all well in the present depressed state of things, and I fear that you will get nothing, if it does.

Yrs &c. J.D. Giles

Rev Dr Giles, Windlesham Hall near Bagshot

Thursday April 21 1859. I received a letter from Sophia, informing me of Maria's death, and the next day came a letter from William containing the same information. I immediately went to Frome, where I met my uncle Captain Giles, and we followed the coffin of my deceased sister to the vault in which my father, mother, and so many of my brothers and sisters are laid on the North-west side of the parish church.

Monday, April 25. I was agreeably surprised at receiving a letter from Thomas Whiting, formerly our groom at Southwick and afterwards at Frome. He first married our housemaid at Frome, Mary Alsop, and tells me he is married again. I annex his original letter, out of respect to his memory and his devoted attachment to myself.

Uphill, April 29th 1859

To Dr Giles Dr Sir

After Much enquirie for several years, I at length procured your address from your Sisters, when I was in Frome a short time since. It is now many years since we last saw each other and many changes doubtless we both have seen both we & ours. I daresay you have a family grown up, and my Daughter Maria when you last saw her a little Girl is now married and has six Daughters living almost close to me. My wife her Mother has been dead about eleven years & you may well suppose I have another and she would be most pleased to see Dr Giles down to Uphill at any time. I am carrying on a very considerable Business and nothing would give me more pleasure than to have Dr Giles as my Guest. I assure you it would be the greatest gratification I could have; your brother Frank once or twice been to see me but his visits were very short, when you come you must make your mind to a good long stay, we shall have so much to say & tell. Please present my best respects to Mrs Giles & Family, hoping sir soon to hear from you I beg to subscribe myself.

yours ever Truly Thos Whitting
Direction: T. Whitting, Merchant, Uphill, Nr Weston Super Mare, Somerset

It will be seen that he signs his name Whitting - I believe because his nephew who became rich and started as a country squire at Uphill, considered Whiting too vulgar; forgetting or perhaps never having known that the last abbot of Glastonbury bore the name of Whiting, and was executed on a charge of treason for not surrendering his abbey to King Henry. Tuesday, June 21. We formed a large pic-nic party and met on Horsington Hill, where we had music and dancing to a great extent. It had been customary with us to have such a party on Arthur's birth-day, and we managed, wherever we were, to keep up the custom. Three of these celebrations were conspicuous above the rest, one in Sir Robert Throgmorton's Park at Buckland, a second on White-horse hill near Uffington, and a third in the ruins of Minster Lovel castle.

Soon after this Herbert and Bayly made a walking tour to High Wycombe and back. Thursday, Sept. 1. Isabella and I, having received an invitation from Lady Durrant, went to spend a week or two at Skottowe Hall in Norfolk. Monday, Sept 19. I went down through Derby to Bristol, where I slept one night at the Saracen's Head, and went on to Burnham, from thence back to Sandford Station where I took what is termed the Marrowbone Stage and got about 8 o'clock to the Firs, where Baldwin Fulford was still alone in his glory. I then started for Bath after a night's repose in a curious old half-tester bedstead belonging to Mrs Collins, and took apartments at No 2 North Parade, the very house where my grandfather Mr John Giles had been with his family during his last illness 66 years before.

Thursday, Sept 29. I wrote a letter to the Daily News, being indignant at the pretentions with which the French began the war against Germany. The Count de Goddes de Liancourt, our old friend, is the hero of my story. On the 3rd of last month he wrote to me - "Good bye! me voila parti pour la malheureuse France! Samedi, 12 pm."

FRANCE AND THE RHINE.
TO THE EDITOR OF THE DAILY NEWS.

SIR, -In your paper of this day you ask whether any man or class of men "rose up anywhere to say that France repudiated all notion of a rectified Rhine frontier, and abhorred as a crime the thought of interfering with the progress of German unification?" I will prepare the way for an answer by an a fortiori argument, which can with difficulty be refuted. If those who were personally as well as publicly hostile to the Emperor and his system on the one hand, and also to their opponents on the other, at once, on the declaration of war, waived their principles and rushed into the fight to gratify national vanity, and to extend the national frontiers, is it not morally certain a fortiori that others who had no such scruples or drawbacks would act in the same manner? The Count de - has resided thirty years in England, and has been connected with me by ties of the closest friendship. He has always hated the Bonapartes and spoken ill of the Emperor. He was already a young man in 1815, and has a vivid recollection of the early triumphs and later disasters of his country. He, in fact, had shaken the dust off his feet against France, and is naturalized in England. No sooner was war declared than he came to bid me farewell. "The war has nothing to do with Spain," said he, "it is for the Rhine. We must have that river for our eastern boundary, and until then France will never be contented." "Perhaps," I replied, "you would like to have the Thames for your northern boundary; it would be just as reasonable. Also the Ebro and the Po towards Spain and Italy." "Oh," said he, "not that; but the Rhine is a good river boundary, which would make peace for ever between the two nations." It was in vain that I showed him that no large navigable river was a boundary between nations, that the Nile, the Danube, the Rhine, the Elbe, Vistula, Peiho, Ganges. Indus, &c., were all highways, and invariably occupied, on both their banks, by the same people. He took his leave, and is at this moment in Paris, from whence we hardly expect to see him emerge again alive; or, if alive, it is to be hoped that he will rejoin his friends in England, at an age verging on seventy, a wiser if not a better man.

I am, &c, TRUTH.

Monday, Oct 3. I went in a van to Lullington Rectory where my old school-master Mr Williams lived, got there just in time to go to bed.

Tuesday, Oct 4. I spent with Mr Williams, and walked through Orchardleigh, where my little brother Edmund was drowned in the lake 50 years ago.

Wednesday, Oct 5. Anna and Ellen joined me at Frome, and we slept at Miss Bull's private hotel. The next day we spent with Aunt Sophia and on Friday, Oct 7, we returned home.

At the end of October I received a letter from the bishop about nominating Mr Bennett &c &c. From the style of it one would suppose that his lordship had discovered Mr Bennett somewhere and directed me to take him. The fact is that our friend Mr Heath found him out for me and I sent him to the bishop, to obtain his approbation, which I knew would pacify the people in the parish, who were going to pay the curate.

Monday, Dec 13. Miss Castendyk, with whom and her sister we had been very intimate at Thun, writes me from Bremen a very nice letter, and in very good English about the war between Germany and France.

Monday, December 20. Baldwin and Isabella Fulford came up from Churchill to spend Christmas with us. He told us of some lady whose bonnet and wig were blown away by a sudden gust of wind on the sea-shore, and a coal-heaver who was standing by showed him a born gentleman by covering her bare head with his own coal-heaver's hat!

Friday, Dec 31. New Year's Eve! ending the year with my usual party of 200.

THE RECTOR'S NEW YEAR'S ENTERTAINMENT. On Friday evening, being New Year's Eve, the rector, the Rev Dr Giles, gave his annual entertainment to about two hundred of his parishioners. One hundred and twenty were invited to tea at eight o'clock, and the table was spread with an abundance of cake, bread and butter, and tea. At nine o'clock there were fifty more admissions and tea went around again. Later in the evening almost every person who came decently dressed was admitted. The company included several of the leading families, among whom may be named Mr and Mrs Collier, Mrs Kydd, Miss H Ruck, Mr Mathewes and his daughters, Mrs Calrow, Mrs and Miss Giles, Mr and Mrs Fulford, Mr Sett, and Mr Carapiet. Mrs Giles and the Misses Mathewes played the piano, and their persevering efforts to entertain the company were most successful. Dancing and singing were kept up with the greatest vivacity till the hour of midnight, and the close of the year 1869, when "God save the Queen" was joined in by all the company. Mr Mathewes, after a few appropriate remarks, proposed to join in a cheer for the rector, which was vociferously responded to, and the entertainment was concluded by an address from the rector, exhorting to the manifestation of those virtues of kindly feelings and benevolence which the season should prominently call forth, and gently recommending and inculcating the exercise of patience to those who at this time find themselves in trouble, difficulty, or privation. He expressed a hope these annual gatherings might not cease till, by a series of invitations, which he trusted would be accepted, he had included everyone of the six thousand inhabitants of Sutton.

1871

Tuesday, June 5. After giving my evidence in the Walrond case I went to Churchill, and began to work as usual in forwarding the repairs and alterations, having no one in the house, but Mrs Kerslake and her son Edward.

Thursday, June 7. I was startled at receiving the annexed telegram, not having heard that my sister had been ill: "Handed in at the Sutton Surrey Office at 9-0am, received here at 10-8am, From A.S. Giles Rectory Sutton, To Rev Dr Giles Churchill Court Bristol, Your sister Mary is Dangerously ill may be dead by this time can you go to Frome."

Friday, June 8. I went to Frome this day and found that poor Mary was dead, and that her funeral was fixed for tomorrow. My eldest sister Sophia informed me that a thoroughly ritualistic ceremony would be gone through, and they began it this night. The body was taken to the church in a procession headed by Mr Bennett the vicar and lay all night at the upper end of the nave, surrounded on all sides by lighted candles standing on candelabra. The members of the Home, a sort of Convent, where Mary had lived under the name of Sister Mary, during the latter years of her life, kept watch one at a time, and each for one hour, near the coffin, and in the morning at 9 o'clock the funeral service was chanted, the candles still burning, and the three or four clergymen, who were present and officiated, swung censers round the coffin and filled the church with the odour of the incense. Mr Bennett the Vicar, who would have been unknown to fame and to the world, but for his tendency to these old-world ceremonies, seemed to me to be much shaken in health, and not likely to preside much longer in the beautiful church, which my brother Charles nominally has restored, but in many of its details may be said to have rebuilt. Immediately after the service, I hastened to the Railway Station and arrived late at Sutton.

Monday, July 2. I lunched with Mrs Jeffery at 22 Cambridge Terrace, whose daughter, married to Mr Evered, had been divorced, and I had promised to marry her again to Mr Badham, if no one else would do so.

Tuesday, July 3. I sent off to Stuckey's Bank Frome my sister Sophia's deeds and to Stuckey's Bank at Bristol the deeds of Arthur's property at Churchill.

Wednesday, July 4. Ellen started for Churchill, and was to meet Isabella starting from Tunbridge with Pedro, at Reading.

Monday, July 9. I received from Stuckey's Frome bank an acknowledgement that they held the deeds of Captain Giles's land, being the security on which my sister Sophia's annuity of £70 a year depends.

Tuesday, July 10. Mr Samler came down and held the usual half-yearly tithe audit at the Greyhound Inn.

Wednesday, July 11. I sent off the old clock to Churchill Court, where one was much wanted, and the same day I went to see Messrs Money Wigram & Co about getting into the service of one of their ships a young scapegrace named Stripp. To my astonishment there is great difficulty in getting boys sent to sea. I used to think the sea-service a gulf into which anyone might plunge; but it appears there is plethora even here.

Thursday, July 12. I received a draft of the conveyance of the Churchill Court estate from Mr Brice.

Tuesday, July 17. I called on Mrs Jeffery in Cambridge Place, and arranged to marry her daughter on Saturday. I then went on to Paddington, and took the train to Stourbridge where I arrived rather late in the evening, and slept in the house, which I had taken for three years as a residence for my brother Frank's widow Eliza.

Wednesday, July 18. I walked with Alice through Hagley, where is Lord Lyttleton's park to Clent, and spent the afternoon very pleasantly with Mr and Mrs Amphlett who is a daughter of Mr Baily a respectable and wealthy manufacturer of Stourbridge. Mr Amphlett is cousin to Judge Amphlett, and his wife was one of the prettiest girls in the neighbourhood, and so fond of my brother, that she was almost inconsolable when he died.

Thursday, July 19. I got released from my tenancy of the house, seeing that Eliza had determined to leave Stourbridge, and I returned to Sutton, calling on my way at 22 Cambridge Terrace, that they might see I should be ready to fulfil my promise on Saturday.

Saturday, July 21. I married Mary Evered alias Jeffery, as promised, at one of the neighbouring churches, stopping to partake of a collation before returning to Sutton.

Parts I & II of the Diary and Memoirs of John Allen Giles appeared in FSLS Yearbooks 17&18 respectively.

I am indebted to David Bromwich and the Somerset Record Society for permission to publish extracts from the diaries. Ed

UNCHRISTIAN CONDUCT OF PUSEYITE CLERGY

The late Thomas Bunn, Esq, so highly respected and much lamented in this town, before his death desired to be interred in the burial place of Christ Church, and that the Rev H Wickham, Incumbent of that Church, should perform the funeral service. Mr Bennett, the Vicar of this town, having some power over the burial green of Christ Church, a note was sent to him by the surviving sister of Mr Bunn, asking, as a favour, the dying request of her brother, but this descendant of the apostles at once refused the boon asked, and to further show his power, ordered the corpse to be brought to St Peter's Church (the other Church not being sufficiently consecrated for the burial service to be read in it), and then carried to Christ Church green, where he performed the service himself; he then left the

grave, leaving one of his Curates there, and whilst hundreds of the inhabitants were anxiously, yet orderly, waiting to pay their last tribute of respect to the deceased gentleman by looking on his coffin, they were prevented doing so, and the grave was ordered to be immediately closed. --- *From a Correspondent.*

Thomas Bunn's Grave

St John's Church was known as St Peter's in 1853. Thanks to ALM for this extract from the Wells Journal 18.V.1853 Ed

Family Roots in Somerset
by Ginny Owen

Like many people I suspect, I started my family history research about 10 years ago, too late to ask many of the people who would have been able to fill in so many of the gaps from their own memories. I was fortunate that my mother had kept all of the more interesting letters and papers that had been found when my paternal grandmother Amy Latham died in 1966 and these were handed over to me when I displayed an interest in tracing the family roots.

One of the more entertaining items was my grandmother's washing book which she had used in order to write down some of her recollections of her family background and her own childhood. It is undated, but the address on the front puts it somewhere in the 1920s. It was from reading this charming account of her early life in the 20th century that I took notice for the first time of my ancestor's connections with Frome and the surrounding area.

I read about Amy's father Thomas Stanley Latham paying visits to his Uncle Thomas Green in Frome in order to spend time with his fiancée Florence Elizabeth Olive. The engagement was necessarily a long one owing to his business ventures in Shanghai having failed twice, leaving him with no way of earning the bread necessary for bringing up a family. In the end Florence's father Edmund Crabb Olive took pity on them and made his daughter an allowance sufficient for the now not-so-young couple to embark on married life.

Armed with these facts and names I was able to start building my family tree. I soon became familiar with more names of notable Frome families; there was so much intermarrying that I came across them many times over. Edmund Crabb Olive was the son of Edward Olive of Frome and Betty Crabb from Tellisford where her family had owned the mill for generations. I have the sampler she sewed in 1792 at Hinton House. Edmund married Eliza Daniel, the daughter of a Bath wine merchant. Her brother Alfred married Eliza Ann Cruttwell and came to Frome as perpetual curate of Trinity Church in the 1830s, later to be Vicar of Holy Trinity. His oldest son Charles Henry Olive Daniel is famous for operating the Daniel Press[1] and followed the family tradition by marrying his cousin Emily Crabb Olive.

Edmund Crabb Olive was an attorney who occupied a prominent position in the town of Frome and the surrounding area. He was at one time agent for the Longleat estate. He went into partnership with Daniel and Cruttwell relatives to form one of Frome's legal practices that has been the subject of an article in a previous Yearbook[2].

It was only a few years ago that I discovered that Frome Museum houses the diaries Thomas Green kept from 1840 until his death in 1882. The most interesting of his writings is a series of Memoranda that he wrote as he went on his travels around England as a young man in the 1820s. The third of these is a visit to the West Country in 1827 when he meets his cousin Jane Sinkins for the second time and is clearly falling deeply in love. The later diaries are more prosaic affairs and will take many years to transcribe in full but the labour is proving worthwhile as more and more snippets of information come out and contribute to the picture of life in Frome 150 years ago.

Uncle Tommy Green, as he was known to his great nieces and nephews, was originally from Nottingham, the son of a lace maker who must have prospered as Thomas was able to retire before the age of 40. He chose Frome as his new home town because it was the native place of his wife and cousin Jane Sinkins, daughter of James Sinkins and Jane Hine[3] who ran a successful draper's business inherited from James' father John. James died young in 1811 but his widow Jane and his son John carried on the business and continued to thrive. John Sinkins married Eliza Stancomb from Trowbridge, daughter of another wealthy clothier, and they lived at Wallbridge House opposite the site of the railway station. He supplemented his already considerable wealth by selling some of his land to the railway company in the 1840s. The house survives on Wallbridge today though without its once extensive gardens but its frontage is nevertheless still a fine example of a house in the Adam style.

The Olives and Daniels are exceptional among the families in this part of my tree for being established church; most of them and those with whom their sons and daughters found partners were staunch Congregationalists. Thomas Green attended the Zion Chapel which was near his home on South Parade. He saw various ministers come and go including William Fernie who arrived in 1839. This somewhat ill-fated man lost his wife in 1845, two children in 1848 and 1849 and then died himself in 1850 aged 36, leaving a widow with two young stepchildren. She stayed in her adopted town, possibly relying on the generosity of people like the Greens and Sinkins.

It is the stories about real people which bring a time and place alive and I am discovering such stories all the time as I continue my research. I shall always have a special fondness for Frome and however many times I manage to snatch a fleeting visit it will not be enough to allow me time for everything I would like to explore.

1 *The Daniel Press, Hilary Daniel, FSLS Yearbook 16, 2013*
2 *A Short History of Daniel & Crutwell, Solicitors, Frome, 1838-1943, FSLS Yearbook 8, 2002*
3 *Jane Sinkins née Hine, Margery Hyde, FSLS Yearbook 19, 2016*

Extracts from Thomas Green's diaries are to be published in future FSLS Yearbooks. Ed.

A section of the Hine Family Tree

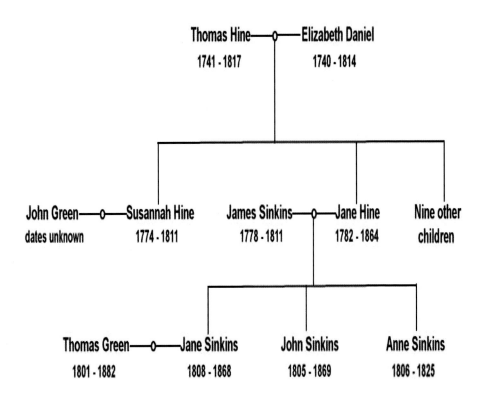

Thomas Hine——○——Elizabeth Daniel
1741 - 1817   1740 - 1814

John Green——○——Susannah Hine   James Sinkins——○——Jane Hine   Nine other
dates unknown   1774 - 1811   1778 - 1811   1782 - 1864   children

Thomas Green——○——Jane Sinkins   John Sinkins   Anne Sinkins
1801 - 1882   1808 - 1868   1805 - 1869   1806 - 1825

Jane Sinkins née Hine 1782 - 1864
by Margery Hyde

Jane Hine, the daughter of Thomas and Elizabeth (née Daniel) Hine, was born in Beaminster, Dorset in 1782. She was the tenth of their eleven children. Thomas Hine was a cloth maker and brewer and his wife was a descendant of the royalist, James Daniel, who fought in the Monmouth rebellion. The Hines were a family of entrepreneurs and this ability was certainly passed on to Jane Hine. Her brother, Thomas, at the age of sixteen was sent to France and ultimately took over his father-in-law's cognac company and renamed it Thomas Hine & Co. The company still trades today. Another brother, Jonathan, became a hosier in Nottingham. An older sister, Susannah, married a lace-maker, John Green also of Nottingham, and their son, Thomas, would later marry Jane's daughter, also Jane. Meanwhile, in October 1804 Jane Hine, married James Sinkins a draper from Frome whose business had been founded by his father. James Sinkins was the son of John and Sarah Sinkins whose home and business were located in Cheap Street.

Jane Sinkins

John Sinkins Sr is described as a Linen Draper but this is a term that, at that time, could cover a multiplicity of activities. Linen was the cloth worn next to the skin and was the material that would have been most in demand. However he would also have traded in wool, silk, ribbon, lace and anything for which there would have been a market. Additionally, it is known that many linen drapers would commission the manufacture of their own cloth from weavers based in homes which were owned by the draper. It is likely that John Sinkins Sr was in this category.

Despite the decline in the wool trade, the Sinkins family were relatively prosperous. At the time of the marriage, James Sinkins settled £1000 (the equivalent today of at least £76,000) in trust on his new wife. Little is known about James Sinkins, although in 1810 he is recorded as representing the trustees of the proposed Zion Independent Chapel in land negotiations. At his death, his will makes clear the extent of this prosperity. In addition to the business he bequeathed further property in Cheap Street plus land and premises in The Butts.

The marriage produced a son (John) and two daughters (Jane and Anne) but James Sinkins died in June 1811 aged 45. Jane Sinkins was left with three small children and the business. The family lived at 7 Cheap Street and the shop was located in the Market Place at what is now the site of HSBC Bank. The shop and two other premises in Cheap Street were leased from Lord Cork under an arrangement whereby the Sinkins family could (and did) sublet to their own tenants and could pass the lease on to their descendants. This arrangement added to the income already derived from the shop and wool trade.

Jane Sinkins chose to carry on the business and, rather than appoint a manager, remained directly involved in it. This was at a time where it was still thought unseemly for a lady to be knowledgeable of business although the expansion in consumerism meant that many women were moving into the retail market usually as milliners or dressmakers. The business in Frome continued to flourish under the title of Jane Sinkins & Son. It seems remarkable that she should have elected to change the name to her own and it would suggest a high level of independent spirit. An interesting contrast is with the life of Jane Bunn who was almost a direct contemporary in Frome. Jane Bunn and her sister Susanna kept diaries of their daily life (now held by Frome Museum) and these record an uneventful existence very much focused on family, friends and church. Neither of the Bunn sisters seems to have generated any initiative of their own.

Mrs Sinkins, however, had no such inhibitions and became an active trader in her own right in the town. Whilst the industrial revolution was raging, very little silver or copper coinage had been issued since the reign of George II. In 1811, in response to this lack of coinage, a group of traders in Frome gathered together to produce trade tokens. Mrs Sinkins was among them and her name is clearly displayed on each token alongside other traders who included a tallow chandler, a grocer and four other grocers who were also wine and spirit merchants. These circulated until the practice was made illegal in 1813.

It would appear that Mrs Sinkins was a force to be reckoned with. In 1818 the town constable, Isaac Gregory, records that Mrs Sinkins had complained that a standing post had been placed in front of her door and prevented its use. Mr Gregory got help and removed the post but the bailiff of the market then censured him for interfering and removing Lord Cork's property as Lord Cork owned the market rights. However, there is no record that the post was moved back suggesting that both bailiff and constable feared the wrath of Mrs Sinkins more than that of Lord Cork. (It may have helped that the Gregory family were neighbours in Cheap Street.)

It is known that Jane Sinkins's son, John, was in a business partnership with his mother. However, in 1830 the year of his marriage to Eliza Stancomb of Trowbridge this partnership was dissolved and John Sinkins had no more direct involvement with the shop and, in later life, he was known to be ashamed of its retail origins. Instead he formed a partnership with a cousin who then ran the shop himself. Instead he became a prosperous mill owner in Frome.

In 1837 Jane Sinkins eventually moved from Cheap Street to South Parade House (which included outhouses, stables and a coach house) at a time when South Parade was considered a very fashionable address. Her daughter and son-in law had lived with her in Cheap Street and moved with her to South Parade. Her business acumen must have allowed her to profit for she started to acquire a property portfolio of her own. In addition to South Parade House she already owned a farm near Ilminster. Later, in 1840, she bought No 6, South Parade and then bought 13-15 Sheppards Barton. She also acquired a site in Rook Lane, a plot opposite South Parade House and three houses in Wine Street. Additionally, the

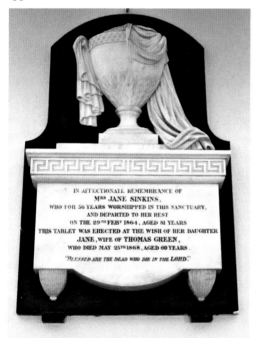

diary of her son-in-law, Thomas Green, records their joint purchases of shares on the Stock Market and they seem to have worked closely together on financial matters. Nevertheless, her spirit of independence evidently lasted until she died. In her own will, she leaves property to her daughter 'for her sole use and benefit independent of any husband she may have but with the power to will it to whomsoever she pleases'.

Jane Sinkins died in 1864 leaving South Parade House to her daughter, Jane Green. There is a plaque to her in the United Reformed Church in Whittox Lane (formerly Zion Congregational Chapel).

Plaque in Zion Chapel   Photo: Diane Rouse

FROME BUILDINGS No 19

Marchants House

Marchants House stood on the corner of Merchants Barton and Church Street until it was demolished for access to Saxonvale in 1970. It was the home of the Marchant family who gave their name to Merchants Barton. The northern facade, a drawing of which appeared in FSLS Yearbook 18, displays another example of Frome's fine 18th century buildings demolished for road widening and 'improvement'. Marchants House contained an outstanding plaster ceiling, which was saved by Elizabeth Stephenson, co-founder of the Bradford on Avon Preservation Trust, who stopped the demolition of the building so that the ceiling could be expertly removed. It has been attractively installed in the Priory Barn at Bradford on Avon. The other Jacobean plaster ceiling in Frome in Monmouth Chambers, 3 Cork Street was saved by Dorothy Brown 20 years ago.

Some of the peculiar roofscape of the old vicarage coach house and outbuildings can still be seen from Church Street looking towards the Silk Mill in Merchants Barton.

Extract from 'Farthing Bundles', the autobiography of
Clara Grant

Clara Grant

I am one of those Wiltshire moonrakers of whom the world is not supposed to hear any more, but, deep down in our hearts, we allow our ancestral story to comfort us with the faith that " we hain't such vools as we do look."

North and South Wiltshire, known of old as the "cheese" and the "chalk," are thus summed up by an old writer, John Aubrey : "According to the several sorts of earth in England (and so all the world over) the indigenae are respectively witty or dull, good or bad. In North Wiltshire (a dirty clayey country) the aborigines speake drawlinge ; they are phlegmatique, skins pale and livid, slow and dull, heavy of spirit; hereabout is but little tillage or hard labour; they only milk the cowes and make cheese; they feed chiefly on milke meates, which cools their braines too much, and hurts their inventions. These circumstances make them melancholy, contemplative, and malicious ; by consequence whereof come more law suites out of North Wilts, at least double to the southern parts. And by the same reason they are generally more apt to be fanatiques ; their persons are generally plump and feggy ; gallipot eies, and some black ; but they are generally handsome enough.

Contrariwise on the Downes, Etc., the south part, where 'tis all upon tillage, and where the shepherds labour hard, their flesh is hard, their bodies strong. Being weary after hard labour, they have not leisure to read or to contemplate of religion, but goe to bed to their rest to rise betime the next morning to their labour."

Chapmanslade. Happily for me I was born in the chalky South, at Chapmanslade, a village standing in two counties, two dioceses and five parishes, the latter facts accounting perhaps for its rather forlorn religious history.

The origin of its name is unknown and its early history uncertain, but it was probably settled by Flemish weavers brought from Flanders in Queen Elizabeth's reign to assist in the manufacture of the famous West of England cloth. I can remember the last of the village weavers, Jack Gore, working at his large handloom in his wide cottage window.

My ancestors being simple country folk kept few family records, but an old chest, dated 1606, was brought by the Grants when they came south from Scotland to work in the forests at Longleat, the famous seat of the Marquis of Bath.

(We like to think that General Grant, the American President, belonged to us, his folk having also come south from Scotland before migrating to the States.)

In these days of educational advantages it is interesting to look back upon the struggles our forebears made in their pursuit of learning, and, viewing the elaborate apparatus and methods devised by the modern infants' teacher for teaching small children to read, it is refreshing to recall how much was achieved of old by simpler means.

Education is, to me, the creation of the right hungers. Our ancestors possessed the hunger and had to forage for their food. In modern days we tend to provide ample food whilst stifling the appetite, and thus there are many who starve in the midst of plenty.

An aunt of mine (later, one of the unofficial pedagogues of the village) recalls the little dame school (the type so vividly described by Crabbe the poet) kept in a cottage by a poor old soul with a cripple husband, and her chief memory is of "Bounce Open Day" at Christmas time, when each pupil took a huge log of firewood and hurled it at the school door which, duly prepared for the attack, bounced open, and thus did the old lady supplement her scanty income.

I remember the postman bringing the letters from Westbury, spending the day at some industry in the village, and walking back at night, sounding his horn for us to bring our letters out as he passed. In my mother's day the postman worked at tailoring with her uncle, and had his dinner with my grandmother, who got him to put some writing copies in books for her children, and, my mother adds, " there were some very good morals in them." Like the family Bible, the oak beam of a cottage ceiling was often found useful for recording family dates.

My mother remembers many books in her home, and her grandfather Biggs was one of three residents sharing *The Times,* costing then 7d by post.

Later on the National School at Corsley was opened and was taught by an old schoolmaster with one leg, who used to run round the school shouting " Give over tah'ken! " (talking).

Multiplication tables were dictated by a "good scholar" standing on a stool, and were accompanied by certain violent physical jerks, very warming. One aunt was reputed to have mastered as far as 12x12, but, as the little monitor always said "Twice 1 *or* 2" she wondered to the end what it all meant.

My father at the age of nine gave a chum 3d for an arithmetic book which he studied hard during breakfast time, munching his toast at the window to get the light, and to the end of his life he was an omnivorous reader. (At seventy he reread both the Bible and Shakespeare.)

His great passion, however, was music. A cousin having taught him his notes, he and a boyfriend got leave to practise on the wheezy old Baptist organ. For six months my father "blew" and his friend played, then they changed places, and it was soon clear that it was not worthwhile for my father to "blow" again, and at fourteen he became organist at the little chapel.

Organ-blowing was regarded as a vital part of the playing, as indeed it was, and one proud mother, dilating to my uncle on her son's success after a few lessons, said, "But then, you know, 'e blowed the organ zix months avore that."

It was not until I was five years of age that Chapmanslade's own National School was opened. No suitable site could be found until a fire destroyed a cottage, from which large baskets of newly laundered clothes were rescued by neighbours, and my eldest brother, then not three, remembers vividly the beautifully goffered cotton sunbonnets rolling gaily up the hill in the wind, my mother chasing them.

Of that little school I was one of the first pupils. Our schoolmaster, Daddy Irons, was a tall, stooping, grey-haired man with sharp features: a lonely old man with a sad domestic history. In his garden grew apples of a specially sweet, pale yellow kind, useful as wages to boys pulling up his weeds or fetching his daily beer. Often on a Saturday he would cross over to our house with a lapful of apples for his "little Clarrie" (I being his pet), and my mother would then make them into dumplings and send me over with them.

I was six when I committed my first act of rebellion against the established order of things. Daddy insisted on our taking five whole minutes over each line in our copybooks. It seemed to me an unwarranted waste of time and I surreptitiously worked in an extra line, for which Daddy, not inclined to birch me, "kept me in." On another occasion, having scratched me accidentally with his birch on its way to somebody else, he consoled me with half of one of the famous apples.

Chapmanslade Congregational Chapel

81

Logbooks in those days were serious documents and entries had to be made daily, even though, as on most days, nothing happened. Among Daddy's entries read by me many years later I found the following :

"The work of the school going on favourable" "The time for attendance is better and the school visited by the Reverend the Curate." "The elder children are required by the Parish on the garden work." "The number of attendances has improved as some has returned from work." "A small attendance this morning as the caravans of a wild beast show passed through the village." (Wise children !) And then, alas ! comes the painful verdict of H M I, (true of so many of us) that "Mr Irons is more vigorous than successful as a disciplinarian." No wonder he once sent for my mother to act as his deputy with one of her own flock!

Religious Life. It was only in the year of my birth (1867) that the little church of SS Philip & James was opened, but there were two chapels; the "Upper" Baptist and the "Lower" Congregational.

I found amongst my father's papers a document dated 1827, containing a poignant appeal for funds to the "Managers of the particular Baptist Fund " in London:

"We enjoy our publick meetings constant and regular by our beloved Pastor and though we have no additions the past year yet we hope there are some amongst us that are asking the way to Zion with their faces thitherwards. We are all in general poor labouring people with familys principly employed in the woollen manufactory in which there is such a increase of machinery that has occasioned such a decrease of manual labour that we are reduced to such a state of penury that we can give but very little towards the support of the ministry and at the same time be honourable in the world" " . . . " We remain your poor unworthy but affectionate and obligated Brethren."

> William Eacott, Pastor
> John Watts
> Anthony Wilkins
> William Holloway
> James Minty

Later on, in the '40s, there came a remarkable minister named Leask, who wrote his "Struggles for Life," in which Chapmanslade is described as "poor, beautiful, romantic Willowfield round which the gentle willows bend by the brooks, like so many patient anglers with their rods." He, too, started a school for boys in his largest room, being "paid in potatoes and cheese."

He describes the excitement caused at the post office and general shop by the arrival of his packets of proofs and the guesses made as to their contents. "Was it a summons from Government?" "Were they railway shares, because if so they would all be ruined." Mr Leask became a DD and died in London in 1884.

His book gives a vivid picture of the spiritual destitution of the village and of his own ardent efforts among his people, the fame of which reached the neighbouring rector officially responsible for its spiritual welfare. Eventually a curate arrived and paid a series of calls involving acute doctrinal controversy, and incidentally we find one of those curious libels on the Church of England of which she has had, perhaps, more than her share. Pressed to visit a poor man who had fallen from a high building, the harassed curate pulled out his prayer book and, turning over its leaves, said: "No, I must decline at present. I find there is no prayer here for broken ribs."

In my young days the Baptists were "served" by local preachers, one Benny P being quite a character. " Dooin'tee go to sdeep, Vred " he would call out. Driving from Warminster he passed the turnpike at Thoulstone Farm, through which, if alone and on ministerial business, he could pass free. Preaching once on " Enter ye in at the stray-it gate" he said: "I doant mean thic there gate down Dolls'on that when I and my wife do come droo on a Zunday morning she do get down and walk zoo that we wunt pay the toll." I think it was he, too, who, in thanking my father and his choir for a selection from the *Messiah,* including "Why do the nations so furiously rage together?" with its runs and trills, said: "We be grateful to the choir for comin' but we diden know they wur com in' to zing comic zongs !" In another village when one of my father's soloists was greeted with "Encore! Encore!" an old man sang out: "What be 'ee making all that noise vor ? Let 'er zing it again."

During the reign of one "Lower Chapel" minister, who refused to resign even when his hearers had dropped to his wife and the chapel cleaner, the Upper and Lower congregations achieved a happy union " in love and fellowship," but on the arrival of a worthier pastor the division again took place. A pathetic letter on the Upper Chapel door in 1928, bemoaning the dwindling numbers, would seem to suggest that union might again be sought with benefit to all. In these days, when probably few congregations in town or country could illuminate each other on their points of unity or divergence, they might all do well to commence each service with their Master's prayer " That they all may be one."

Being rather delicate after we removed to Frome, I paid long visits to my native village, and I love to recall old friends, their words and their little tales. Parish Pay was half-a-crown per week, and I remember shopping for old Ann-Noah (so frequent was intermarriage that a wife's Christian name made a convenient prefix to her husband's). The old lady's order ran "½d. o' Tay (tea), ½d. Tyape, ½d. o' Writin' pyaper and a ½ lb. of Vat Byacon." Total 2d. Fat bacon was a great stand-by for supper, and one old lady replied to her husband's " Lah, Ann, how thy tongue doo hring," "Well, and han't I just well greased 'un?"

Blancmange was a novelty, and my uncle, serving it at a Club supper, was asked: "See 'ere, is that pudden or lard?" Sweets were "pops," a mole was a "want," a rat was a "hrot," to bother was to "caddie," to be cold was to be "shrammed," and to have "spreathed hands," but I only once heard "housen" for houses. "Look-zee at 'e, a lookin' at I," said a Frome woman recently at an outdoor meeting. We may, perhaps, smile at the "look-zee," but, for the few who seem able to see without looking, there are all too many who look and do not see, so there may be value in the double appeal.

Broad dialect as I remember it must inevitably die out, but it has a directness and a picturesqueness all its own and is worth preserving, if only by the few who love it.

Astronomical discoveries were received with scorn. "You tell I that anybody do know the zize and weight of they stars ? 'Tis all lies. The zize of the stars, indeed. Have anybody ivir bin up there to measure 'em ? " " What do 'em say, that the earth do goo round the zun ? Then if thic hawk zeed a mouse down under 'en, by the time 'e got down to'en thic mouse'd be over to Short Street."

Surplices were unknown until the opening of the little church. There being no school and the vestry being small, the " robing " took place at our house, and the solemn procession of white-robed clergy and choir struck fear into at least one heart. " They do look like angels. Is it the Judgment Day a-comin' ? " The feeble tinkle of the two church bells, however, could scarcely be mistaken for the Last Trump.

Children and even grown-ups were afraid of seeing ghosts in the chapel burial ground, but my mother remembers her grandfather's consoling logic: "Ghosts can't possibly return to earth since if people were good and went to heaven they would never wish to return to this life, whilst those who went to the wicked place the bogey man would see that they never came back."

Life was simple and natural, but it was narrow. Chapmanslade is still as cut off from the railway as when two of my uncles walked three miles to Westbury and three back from Frome for the novelty of a ride in the train between the two towns, but it has now motor buses, its Memorial Hut, its Women's Institute, though it has as yet no Cinema, and alas ! no resident clergyman.

I have dwelt on these early memories because they account for a habit of mine which puzzles London teachers. I had, in those days, two great yearnings: to be a teacher and to live in London. From a certain hilly spot I used to gaze longingly at a wide view with the smoke of a town on the horizon. "That may be Bath," I used to say, " but at least London is next." Long years after I spent one memorable and crowded day in the city of my dreams. We saw all its biggest sights and glories, but the one impression I took back with me was that of the streaming multitude of London's citizens crossing and recrossing London Bridge and never a sign of recognition! I once heard the late Dr Rudolf Steiner explain why the first seven years of life matter so much. In our later years we pursue selected interests with varying parts of our being, with divided forces as it were. In our early years we embrace and assimilate impressions and experiences with the whole of our being, and that is why our first environment of right manners, habits, speech, religion, relationships (as distinct from informative lessons) are so important, because lasting.

I owe to my village childhood that instinct for intimate personal friendships which make " living near school " neither unnatural nor supernatural, as some would have it, but just natural and inevitable. It is a joy to greet and be greeted in our own streets, to be escorted by cheery children in my goings out and comings in, to meet in a seaside teashop our friendly dustman, and to have my bus ticket from Victoria Station handed to me without asking for it, with a kindly " You're a long way from 'ome, Miss Grant."

Life, at its richest, is the fine art of relationships, widening, as well as deepening, as the years roll on.

Clara Grant was born on the 21 June 1867 at 82, High Street, Chapmanslade and the family moved to 6, North Parade, Frome in 1875. She became a Teacher and founded the Fern Street Settlement in Bromley-by-Bow. She introduced many modern methods of teaching and was created O B E in 1949, the year of her death. Ed

A Happy Ending

Frome Society Yearbook 14 included the story[1] of a scrapbook found, rather mysteriously, in Kingston Deverill. Research showed that the book belonged to a Miss Charlotte Sulivan, a wealthy and well connected mid-Victorian lady who lived in Fulham. We are pleased to draw this story to a happy conclusion. The scrapbook has been acquired by the Faringdon Collection Trust on behalf of Lord Faringdon, the senior member of Charlotte's family.

[1] *Secrets of the Linen Press by Owen Dicker and Margaret Nuth, FSLS Yearbook 14, 2011.*

Mr Gladstone comes to Frome
by Peter Clark

On the morning of Monday 22 January 1877 William Ewart Gladstone, former and future Prime Minister, came to Frome. He spent an hour here and spoke to a crowd of fans outside the railway station.

In the next few pages I wish to explore the background of that visit, the political background of the duel between Gladstone and Benjamin Disraeli, the local context, the people Gladstone met in and around Frome and the legacy of the visit.

Gladstone had been Prime Minister of a reforming Liberal government from 1868 to 1874 when the Conservatives came to power under the leadership of Benjamin Disraeli. From 1852 Gladstone and Disraeli had been increasingly bitter rivals, alternating first as Chancellor of the Exchequer and then as Prime Minister. They were of contrasting backgrounds. Gladstone was from a Liverpool commercial family, was educated at Eton and Christ Church Oxford and was driven by a devotion to the Church of England. Disraeli was from an immigrant Jewish family that had converted to Christianity. His grandfather came to England from Venice. Disraeli had had a raffish and foppish youth; he was the last of the Regency bucks, writing fashionable novels and composing epigrams. (Disraeli is more represented in dictionaries of quotations than any other Prime Minister.) Both were outsiders in the aristocratic world of British politics, but both, in different ways, identified with the ruling classes. Both believed in the importance of aristocratic government. Both liked to have a Duke or two in their cabinets. Both were great orators, appealing to people outside that small world of the upper classes. Both had hinterlands of intellectual activity: Disraeli as a novelist and Gladstone as a writer on theology and the classics. Both were all their lives compulsive scribblers, Disraeli as an elegant writer of letters to elderly ladies, Gladstone as a diarist.

Gladstone *Disraeli*

86

Their rivalry was part of the great drama of Victorian politics. Their contrasting personalities led to a mutual loathing. Their varying approach to Queen Victoria was revealing. Gladstone revered the institution of monarchy but he was never able to unbend in the presence of the Queen. Disraeli employed charm and flattery and won her over to many of his policies. *Her* affection for Disraeli reflected an intense dislike for Gladstone.

After losing the General Election in 1874, Gladstone resigned the leadership of the Liberal Party, wishing for an interval for religious contemplation between office and the grave. The Party in parliament was led by two aristocrats, Lord Hartington, heir to the dukedom of Devonshire, and Lord Granville. It is, in retrospect, hard to believe his intentions for he was to become Prime Minister another three times in the following twenty years, finally retiring at the age of eighty-four. But he did sell his house in Carlton House Terrace, geographically convenient for the House of Commons, and take another house a mile or so away in Harley Street. Disraeli believed the retirement was genuine, for he too withdrew from the House of Commons, becoming in the summer of 1876 the Earl of Beaconsfield. He called it <u>Beaco</u>nsfield, and not Beaconsfield because he wanted to be a <u>beacon</u> to the younger generation.

During that summer of 1876 the political climate was transformed. For the previous two years there were uprisings in the Christian Balkan provinces of the Turkish Ottoman Empire. In June and July 1876 reports of a ferocious repression by Turkish irregular troops in Bulgaria reached Britain. At first Disraeli dismissed the reports as coffee-house bawble. In one of his last statements to the House of Commons he refused to believe some of the alleged atrocities, including the claim that 10,000 people had been thrown into prison. *I doubt whether there is prison accommodation for so many, or that torture has been practised on a great scale on an oriental people who seldom, I believe, resort to torture, but generally terminate their connection with culprits in a more expeditious manner.* These reports of atrocities led to a campaign in Britain that was targeted against Disraeli who was seen as being cynically indifferent to Christian suffering, and being complacent if not complicit with the Ottoman perpetrators of atrocities. The campaign led to an extraordinary and unprecedented series of popular protests in many parts of Britain. If unprecedented, there were some parallels during the previous eighty years. In the first decade of the century Evangelical Christians under the leadership of William Wilberforce pioneered a popular protest against the slave trade. In the 1830s and 1840s the Chartist movement demanded a raft of democratic measures. In the 1840s an organised campaign throughout the northern counties of the country led to the repeal of Corn Laws that had protected the rural interests.

In June and July there were meetings, often initiated by prominent Nonconformist Ministers, up and down the country. At first Gladstone was not involved but during August he stirred himself into activity. He threw off his apparent retirement. Although bedridden with an attack of lumbago he nonetheless wrote a pamphlet with the title, *Bulgarian Horrors and the Question of the East* in just three days. It became one of the most successful political pamphlets in British history, selling 40,000 copies in the first week of its publication on 6 September 1876 and 200,000 by the end of the month. In it he called for the removal of the Ottoman officials from Bulgaria. In ringing tones that echo to our day, his written words reflected his oratory:

Let the Turks now carry away their abuses in the only possible manner, namely by carrying off themselves. Their Zaptiehs and their Mudirs, their Bimbashis and their Yuzbashis, their Kaimakams and their Pashas, one and all, bag and baggage, shall I hope clear out from the province they have desolated and profaned.

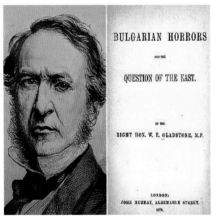

The Bulgarian Horrors Pamphlet

It is worth noting that Disraeli and Gladstone had both visited the Ottoman Balkans. Their experiences had been characteristically very different. Disraeli had been on a tour of the Near East in his youth. He was romantically seduced by the Ottoman Empire and for one melodramatic moment considered enrolling in the Ottoman army to assist in the suppression of a revolt in 1831. Gladstone had been on a mission to Corfu in 1859 and crossed over briefly to Albania where a muezzin was induced to deliver a call to prayer for his personal benefit even though it was not the time for the call to prayer.

Their reaction to the events in the wider political picture differed. Gladstone was selectively fired by causes which he made into a moral campaign. Earlier in his life it had been Italian unification. In his last decades it was Home Rule for Ireland. Now it was the oppression of Christians in the Ottoman Balkan provinces. By contrast Disraeli saw the Ottoman Empire as a potential ally of Britain, another Muslim Empire alongside Britain's Muslim Empire in India.

Gladstone actually sent a complimentary copy of the pamphlet to Disraeli, now Lord Beaconsfield, at his home at Hughenden near High Wycombe. Beaconsfield's immediate reaction was contemptuous: *vindictive and ill-written – that of course. Indeed of that respect of all the Bulgarian horrors perhaps the greatest.*

Throughout the latter half of 1876 Britain was stirred by a public campaign urging the government to act tough with the Ottoman Empire. Public demonstrations were held throughout the country. The campaign was initially driven by a young journalist from Darlington, W T Stead, and climaxed in a great Convention at St James's Hall London in December. In the 19th century parliament generally met only between January and August. This reflected the landed classes' preoccupations, for after August the pre-democratic political classes were mainly concerned with harvest, hunting and house parties. Rarely was Parliament summoned in the autumn months. With a growing popular interest in politics and public affairs, the autumn became the season for agitation. Towns and villages sent petitions to the Secretary of State for Foreign Affairs, the Earl of Derby, and people of Frome actually sent one of the largest and most elaborate. The pattern of protest reflected Nonconformist England, the south-west as much as anywhere else in the country. Gladstone himself observed that *the rural and Tory counties of Wiltshire and Somerset were as sound and as warm in the Eastern Question as the North and North East.*

This was democracy asserting itself. There were precedents for this kind of extra-parliamentary agitation. But the Bulgarian agitation reflected a foreign affairs issue, with people expressing a moral outrage about what they saw as a pusillanimous response on the part of the British government to atrocities overseas. As a popular campaign it anticipated campaigns against the Suez war in 1956 and the demonstrations against the Iraq war in 2003.

Meanwhile the government, after affecting disinterest, responded to public feeling by taking part in an international conference in December 1876 at Constantinople with the object of encouraging reforms in the Ottoman Empire. The British representative was the Marquis of Salisbury, later Prime Minister. He travelled slowly and unenthusiastically across Europe. He was not confident. For him such a trip meant *seasickness, much French, and failure.*

The 1876 public campaign, like the later ones, split families and challenged older loyalties. Paradoxically Nonconformist England had allies from the other end of the spectrum of English Protestantism: High Church Anglicans. I say English Protestantism, for Scotland took little part, and there were not many Catholics in the campaign. The main support for the agitation was Liberal and Nonconformist but there were quite a few dissident Conservatives, one of the most significant being the fourth Marquis of Bath, of Longleat. This Lord Bath had travelled much in Europe and in the 1860s had been Ambassador to Portugal. He had inherited his title as an infant and usually supported the Conservative interest in Frome. He was a High Churchman and had sponsored the Tractarian Vicar of Frome, the Reverend W J E Bennett. He had been close to the Conservative Party leadership and two years earlier, in 1874, had entertained Disraeli, as Prime Minister, at Longleat.

The 4th Marquis of Bath

Disraeli arrived at Longleat, having travelled from Queen Victoria's Isle of Wight residence, Osborne. It was a grim journey by train, with delays at Southampton and Salisbury. At Salisbury, he wrote in a letter to one of his lady friends: *I found Lady Paget* [of Cranmore], *who was going to Longleat with her son, a very young Etonian. I could not avoid giving her a place in my compartment, and she talked, with her usual cleverness, the whole way: an hour of prattle on all subjects. We did not get to Longleat till 9, and though we dressed in ten minutes, people who dine at 8 don't like dining at 9. I sat by Lady Bath but, with a racking headache, rare with me, and not in very good spirits. . . . A more insipid, and stupid, and gloomy dinner I never assisted at, and I felt conscious that I added my ample quota to the insipidity and the stupidity and the gloom. Lady Paget tried to rally the scene, but she had exhausted her resources between Salisbury and Warminster.*

The disillusion seems to have been mutual for Lord Bath later described Mr Disraeli as *the dullest guest he ever entertained at Longleat.*

The following day Disraeli came to Frome. It must be remembered that, insofar as Disraeli had any religious views, he was a Low Churchman, hostile to the ritualism and High Churchmanship of Lord Bath and the Vicar of Frome, Mr Bennett, but he graciously accepted an invitation to come here. *Lady Bath drove me to Frome to see Bennett's famous church, with a sanctuary where "lay people" are requested not to place their feet, and among other spiritual pageantry, a Calvary, and good sculpture. The church is marvellous; exquisitely beautiful, and with the exception of some tawdriness about the high altar, in admirable taste.*

Politics in Frome reflected politics in the capital, with rival aristocratic interests sponsoring the main political parties. The Baths were Conservative, and the Earls of

Cork of Marston were Whiggish Liberals. Lord Bath supported the Conservative parliamentary interest in the General Election of 1874, and helped to unseat the sitting Liberal MP, Thomas Hughes, the author of *Tom Brown's Schooldays*. The new Conservative MP for Frome, Henry Lopes, did not last long. He was appointed a High Court Judge in 1876, and had to resign as MP, triggering a by-election. It may be that the gaucheness of Disraeli as a Longleat guest two and a half years earlier combined with a hostility to Disraeli's Low Churchmanship, which took legislative form in a Public Worship Regulation Act, led to Lord Bath's disenchantment with Disraeli as Prime Minister. Lord Bath felt closer to Gladstone's religious views and shared with him a concern about Turkish actions in Bulgaria. He was active in support of the atrocities campaign in Somerset and was supported by two other interesting men. One was the historian, Edward Freeman, who lived just outside Wells. He had written on Turkish history but was passionately anti-Ottoman Empire which he denounced as the Empire of Sodom. Another coordinator of the campaign was a man called James Farley who had been a banker in Constantinople. He had written about the Christians and other minorities in the Ottoman Empire and was actually the Turkish Consul in Bristol.

Back to the Frome by-election. Politics was a hot issue in Frome then. One of the local papers, *The Frome Times*, was strong in the Conservative interest. At the operational level beneath the aristocratic patronage, politics was run by leading figures of the town. The Wickhams, the Cruttwells and the Daniels were Anglican and Conservative. The Rawlings, the Flatmans and the Tanners were Nonconformist and Liberal. The Conservative candidate in the by-election was a former Governor of New Zealand and a former Under-Secretary for India, Sir James Ferguson. The Liberal candidate was Henry Samuelson who had also been an MP before. The candidates held meetings in pubs. *The Frome Times* was confident of Conservative victory. *In the next issue of* The Frome Times, it promised, *it will be our pleasure and privilege to offer our hearty congratulations to the Electors of this town upon having selected for their representation a gentleman qualified in all respects to fill this important position.*

The people of Frome had other ideas. Lord Bath was lukewarm in his support for the Conservatives and the Frome electorate turned a small Conservative majority into a small Liberal majority.

The Frome Times was shocked. *The result of the Frome Election*, it declared, *is a mystery which cannot be solved by the ordinary process of ratiocination.* Frome was, it went on, *a very rotten borough.* It blamed new voters *who know nothing and care less about what goes on in the world which extends beyond the sphere of their daily associations.*

Gladstone travelled to the Frome district on Wednesday 17 January 1877 via Bristol. He had celebrated his sixty-seventh birthday three weeks earlier. As he grew older Gladstone often toured the country staying at stately homes, hosted indiscriminately by both Tory and Liberal grandees. Later in life he often combined these progresses with a speaking tour. After railing on behalf of the masses against the classes, he would go to spend the night at a ducal palace or some other stately home. He came to Longleat as the guest of Lord and Lady Bath and stayed five days until the following Monday. Lord Bath had gathered a party of what Gladstone called *Eastern sympathisers*; these included a High Church Canon of St Paul's Cathedral Henry Liddon, and the historian Edward Freeman. Each day Gladstone went to a service at the Longleat chapel. On the Friday he walked over to Shearwater. On the Saturday he recorded in his diary: *Walk about place & park in forenoon; beautiful drive in afternoon to Stourhead. This is a noble place: with a host & hostess who are admirable.*

On the Saturday morning he recorded in his diary that he saw Mr Rawlings. Now this man was actually the leader of the Gladstone supporters in Frome. This meeting was clearly to make arrangements for Gladstone's Frome visit.

Samuel Tovey Rawlings was the first secretary of the Frome Liberal Association which was founded in 1875. He was the great-grandson of the founder of the business, Samuel Rawlings and Son. The firm specialised in carding, a trade that was an essential support to the woollen textile industry. Originally teasels that grew in abundance in the area were used to tease out loose fragments of wool. In the 18th century Frome seems to have been a national centre for carding. A teasel appears on the town's coat of arms. In the course of time the teasels were replaced by wire combs, similar to those used for combing dogs today. At the height of their prosperity they were using eighty miles of wire a day. The Rawlings had been a well-established family in Frome for three hundred years. Until the development of machinery the work was labour-intensive and in the 18th century the Rawlings claimed to employ five hundred people. In the 19th century they had a factory next to where the Memorial Theatre is today, and the firm survived there until 1972. The buildings still stand and have been converted by Pang Properties into desirable blocks of flats. The family house, Oriel Cottage, also still stands and is on the corner of Christ Church Street West and South Parade.

By mid-Victorian times the Rawlings family diversified, and manufactured leather belting for driving machinery, and cards for grooming animals. The family prospered and was active in many of the public affairs of the town.

Samuel Tovey Rawlings had a long connection with Badcox Lane Baptist Church where he was a deacon. He was a Poor Law Guardian, and, when the Frome Urban District Council was established in 1894 he, and his brother, Henry Tovey Rawlings, were among the first fifteen members. He had an abiding interest in the Frome Volunteer Fire Brigade and was for many years its captain. When a new fire engine was needed he raised funds through a bazaar opened by Lord Bath's mother and held in the market hall, the building which is now part of the NatWest Bank. Of a mechanical and creative turn of mind he actually invented a new and improved fire escape. This was patented and sold throughout the country and beyond. The Rawlings brothers were archetypal Gladstonian Liberals. As entrepreneurs, wealth creators, public spirited activists representing a Nonconformist conscience, they had more in common with Gladstone's supporters in the north of England than with people of the Home Counties.

S T Rawlings   *H T Rawlings*

Gladstone left Longleat on Monday 22 January after attending a service in Longleat chapel at 9 o' clock. He was expected at Frome railway station at eleven o'clock, and arrived ten minutes late in an open carriage drawn by two bay horses. A temporary platform had been erected in the station yard and there were, according to *The Frome Times*, about 2,000 present: a substantial number bearing in mind that the town's population was about 12,000 then. Were they not at work? Or school? He was accompanied by Mrs Gladstone. The leading aristocratic Liberal, the Earl of Cork, greeted them and escorted them to the station waiting room to meet Mr Rawlings and other leading Liberals. Also present were the son and heir of Lord Cork, Lord Dungarvan, and the recently elected Member of Parliament for Frome, Mr Samuelson.

Carriages waiting at Frome Railway Station

They then came out of the station. Mr and Mrs Gladstone ascended the platform to loud and long cheering. Gladstone, *The Frome Times* reported, *looked remarkably well, and appeared very pleased with his reception.* Mr Samuelson MP then said a few words, followed by Mr Le Gros, President of the Frome Liberal Association, who attributed the recent by-election victory to the feeling on what was called the Eastern Question, and to the writings and speeches of Gladstone. Regardless of the embarrassment that might be given to the new leaders of the Liberal Party, he expressed *our earnest hope that the time may not be far distant when we may again see you at the head of a united Liberal Party, and actively engaged in directing the affairs of the nation.* He then called for three cheers for Mr Gladstone.

Gladstone then stepped forward.

Mr Chairman, Mr Samuelson, and Ladies and Gentlemen, he said. *I am deeply grateful for the kind manifestation of your feelings on this occasion, and I am not less pleased to have an opportunity of congratulating you personally, as I have previously done by letter, upon the great triumph you have recently achieved.* [Applause.] *But I am not on this occasion going to attempt to instruct or inform you on matters of general policy, for this reason, amongst others, that I don't think there is any constituency in England which at present is in less need of instruction.* [Laughter and applause] *I only hope that many will be found to follow your example.* [Hear hear] *...*

In the limited time which is at our disposal before the imperative call of the railway train, I should like to say one word to you upon that subject which at present absorbs almost the entire political sentiments of the country. [Cheers]

I think it is a noble feature in the character of a great people that, upon adequate occasion, it is able to transplant, as it were, the scene of its sympathies and emotions from its own firesides, and from its own domestic exigencies, to the greater and more urgent exigencies of the oppressed in distant lands. [Hear, hear]

He went on to acknowledge that the Frome by-election result was because of concern about the Eastern Question. *I was at one time in hopes, Ladies and Gentlemen, that our good friends, who are also our Conservative opponents, would have followed the admirable example which was set them by your distinguished neighbour, Lord Bath,* [Hear, hear] *and would have vindicated for this great subject of humanity and justice the high station of a national question, in regard to which there is no distinction of party.* [Hear, hear]

Gladstone went on to reply to the request that he resume leadership of the Liberal Party. *I cannot hope to concur with you. . . .With regard to myself, that to which I aspire is that – during the limited time which alone can remain to me, when I have been not much less than half a century in the service of the country – I may be permitted quietly, and I hope really, to serve in the rank and file of the Liberal Party under leaders in whom I have perfect confidence, and who will always do honour to it and themselves.*

Mr and Mrs Gladstone

He concluded, *Let me reiterate my gratitude for the extreme kindness with which you have welcomed me. It has been a great pleasure to me to see a little more of your beautiful country in this portion of Wiltshire and Somersetshire than it has often been in my power to behold; and I shall carry with me, in passing elsewhere, recollections that will never fail, of the free, ready and cordial welcome you have been pleased to accord me.* [Loud and enthusiastic cheers.]

Lord Cork then escorted Mr and Mrs Gladstone to the train, and they left to renewed loud and enthusiastic applause.

Gladstone went on to Wells by train, in time for an afternoon service in the cathedral at 3pm. He stayed at the Bishop's Palace as the guest of the Bishop, Lord Arthur Hervey, whom he had known since they were both boys at Eton together.

The meeting at Frome railway station was one of a series – anticipating the notion of a whistle-stop tour. Gladstone seemed to relish these encounters with the public though he protested in a letter to Lord Granville, that *I have the utmost difficulty in getting rid of the Addresses & invitations, the gatherings at Railway stations and the like.* His truer feelings come through when in the same letter he wrote enthusiastically how *we had a triumphant procession yesterday through the little rural town of Glastonbury headed by a band and flags from a village two miles off, with a long train in the liveliest enthusiasm as they ploughed along through the rain and mud.*

After this burst of enthusiasm for a visiting celebrity Frome resumed its even tenor. The Conference in Constantinople reached no conclusion, but tensions continued in that part of the world. The Ottoman Empire found itself at war with Serbia and with Russia in 1877. Disraeli managed to keep Britain out of it, although he had enthusiastic support to engage on the Ottoman side from all sorts of people, from London theatre goers to the Queen. Just as Gladstone voiced an anti-Turkish sentiment so Disraeli's supporters gave expression to an anti-Russian feeling, a fear that Russia was aspiring to seize Constantinople. The British fleet was on alert in the eastern Mediterranean and in 1878 soldiers of the Indian army were brought to the region. The crisis was ultimately settled in Berlin at a Congress hosted by Bismarck. The Ottoman Empire lost some of its Balkan territories, parts of Bulgaria became independent, but a major international war was averted. Disraeli, the Earl of Beaconsfield, prematurely aged, travelled to the Congress and returned, proclaiming that he had achieved Peace with Honour, and also the annexation of Cyprus to the British Empire. He was rewarded by the Queen by being made a Knight of the Garter.

Meanwhile in Britain Gladstone continued to campaign against what he called Beaconsfieldism. He maintained the pressure on the government and conducted a barnstorming campaign around Edinburgh where he was adopted as parliamentary candidate for the constituency of Midlothian. The Liberals were returned at the General Election in early 1880. Gladstone was still not the leader but it was impossible to ignore him, and the Queen was, with the utmost reluctance, obliged to invite him to form his second government.

In 1879 the Marquis of Bath went to Bulgaria to see for himself and wrote *Observations on Bulgarian Affairs.* Mr Samuelson retained his seat in the 1880 General Election. The Earl of Beaconsfield was seventy-six in 1880. He was frail and died in April 1881. Gladstone was presented with a new dilemma. He hated the man, but had really to pay tribute and racked his brains to find something positive to say about him. Eventually he satisfied his conscience by praising Disraeli's courage – a morally neutral quality.

The events of the late 1870s left ripples that have continued to today. Disraeli's support for the integrity of the Ottoman Empire does not seem so wild today when we contemplate the post-Ottoman history of the Middle East and the Balkan Peninsula. The independent countries of the Christian Balkans look on Gladstone as a hero, and streets are named after him in their capitals.

In Britain the custom of politicians addressing large crowds initiated and developed by Gladstone became a feature of British politics until the television age. His own policies of cutting back public expenditure have been adopted by a fellow Old Etonian, David Cameron and Disraeli's concept of "One Nation" was espoused by a fellow Jew, Ed Miliband. Perhaps Victorian politics were not after all so very different.

This article is based on a presentation during the Frome Festival in 2014 with Derek Wilson as Gladstone, Hilary Daniel as Disraeli and Peter Clark, Narrator. Ed

Frome Market
by David Millard

The first market at the then new agricultural centre at Standerwick took place on Wednesday 28th March 1990.

It is now, therefore, 26 years since the relocation of the Frome Livestock Market from its former site in the centre of the town.

The background to the relocation of the market is well known to all of those who were at the time living in the town or the surrounding area and is covered very comprehensively in Alan Sandall's book 'Going Going Gone' published in June 1991. This article is a very brief record of the changes that have taken place during those 26 years, an indication of the current throughputs of livestock and the status of Frome regionally and nationally as a livestock centre.

Prior to the move the market at Frome, restricted by the space available and the access to the site, was tiny compared to other local and regional centres. The market now handles more livestock in one week than it did throughout the whole year prior to the move.

Frome Market, Standerwick   *Photo: Cooper & Tanner*

The Owners and Operators

The then Partners of Cooper & Tanner had purchased Moors Farm at Standerwick and obtained planning consent for it to be converted into an Agricultural Centre prior to the firm being acquired by Nationwide. The construction of the centre was undertaken whilst owned by Nationwide. Subsequently the Partners of Cooper & Tanner had the opportunity to re-acquire the agricultural business of the firm including the operation of the market. Initially the firm rented the premises from Nationwide but one of the terms agreed between the parties provided for the Tenants to have the option to purchase the freehold, which they exercised.

At the same time the firm entered into an agreement with Ian MacNicol and his family who owned and operated the livestock markets at Yeovil and Sturminster Newton, whereby the freehold was owned in part by the MacNicol family and part by the firm and the livestock operating businesses of the three were merged. The MacNicol family created 'Premier Livestock Auctions' who owned and operated the business with Cooper & Tanner with the two firms then involved at Yeovil and Sturminster Newton acting as Auctioneers.

This arrangement continued successfully and in the meantime Premier Livestock Auctions had acquired the livestock markets of both Chippenham and Avon, but sadly Ian MacNicol died in 2006. In 2013 terms were agreed between the MacNicol family and Cooper & Tanner and Symonds & Sampson for the two firms to take over the market business, renting the premises from the family, and 'Frome Livestock Auctioneers' was formed and continues to carry on the business today.

Livestock Markets and Agriculture

During the past 26 years much has happened. Initially, 5 or 6 weeks after opening the market, there was the scare relating to BSE which for a period adversely affected both the throughput and value of stock. Then for one year, February 2001-February 2002, the livestock market was closed due to the restrictions imposed as a result of the Foot & Mouth outbreak. Very fortunately, there were no cases in the immediate area. More recently restrictions imposed on some farms and the movement of animals as a result of TB have had an effect on throughput levels.

The livestock markets at Sturminster Newton, Yeovil, Chippenham and Avon were all closed and therefore the business concentrated solely on Frome. Many other markets closed during the period, especially those situated on urban sites, including Banbury known as 'the stock market of Europe', Gloucester and many others.

In short, livestock markets just like so many farms and businesses either became larger or ceased trading. Livestock farming is currently experiencing a very difficult period with the price being paid for milk generally below the cost of production, and the value of prime stock stands at reduced levels.

At Frome the major and very spectacular increase in throughput relates to store cattle. The market operates on two days a week, the traditional Wednesdays with prime stock, cull stock, dairy etc and store cattle on Fridays. Friday was, formerly, the principle market day at both Chippenham and Yeovil. Store cattle, animals from between approximately 3 – 18 months old, bred and reared from suckler and dairy herds are sold to buyers from the whole country, largely the north of England, southern Scotland and Wales. During certain seasons of the year over 1,000 store cattle are being sold regularly at Frome every week. Quality, variety and numbers attract buyers many of whom travel great distances to be at Frome.

Throughput of Stock

In 2015 over 100,000 animals were sold at Frome. These numbers comprise 11,300 beef cattle and cull cows, 35,187 lambs and sheep, 10,100 calves, 2,200 dairy cattle and 41,700 breeding and store cattle. The markets regularly attract vendors from Somerset, Wiltshire, Dorset, Devon, Gloucestershire, Hampshire and the Isle of Wight.

Other Activities

As well as the livestock market Cooper & Tanner conduct on a Wednesday weekly antique, fine art, furniture and general sales averaging about 800 lots per week. Seasonal agricultural implement and other sales are held on site and the Conference Centre is used regularly by the firm for Property Auctions. There is a Restaurant and Conference Centre which is used regularly by a number of local organisations. The offices around the market square are all full, both Cooper & Tanner and Symonds & Sampson have offices; and others include Solicitors, Accountants, Insurance Brokers etc. The site is also used for Stalls on a Wednesday and Car Boot Sales on a Sunday.

Store Cattle Auction Ring   *Photo: Cooper & Tanner*

99

The Frome & District Annual Fatstock Show & Sale is held on the first Wednesday in December each year with 200 supporters of the market sitting down to the annual and traditional dinner on the following Friday.

The Present and Future

Frome Livestock Market is operated by Frome Livestock Auctioneers which is chaired by Michael Joyce of Cooper & Tanner with Andrew Robinson of Symonds & Sampson as Vice Chairman.

Whilst the relocation of the livestock market 26 years ago, just as with the Frome Agricultural and Cheese Show 15 years ago, were not universally popular with all Frome residents, there is no doubt that neither would have survived without moving. Few would now doubt that the livestock market in particular having vacated the former site has been to the considerable benefit of the town of Frome enabling the area to be used for numerous other purposes.

Frome Livestock Market is now recognised over a very wide area as being a major agricultural centre whose success mirrors the success of the town in so many other areas.

Mr Haine's Prize Lambs - an old postcard

My Years with the St John's Ambulance Brigade (1942-1949)

by Diana Crossman

I was 11 years old and had just started my first year at Frome Grammar School, taking the bus from Frome Station, since we rented rooms in Victoria Road. Frome was in darkness at night with blackout curtains pinned up, shutters closed, no street lights and all sign posts taken down. We all wore identity discs round our necks; my number was WOFG 393.

Everyone combined to help in the war effort. My father was busy in the evenings waiting for evacuees to arrive from Paddington Station and escorting them to their new homes. Women knitted scarves and gloves for servicemen. Children learnt 'to do their bit' and this is how I got involved. At the end of a French lesson, our friendly teacher, Mr Moran, announced: 'If you are interested in learning about first aid, would you come to the Blue House on Saturday afternoon and hear about St John's Ambulance Brigade?' I liked the idea and told my parents; my father was pleased since he had been an ambulance driver in WW1.

I walked to the Blue House at 2pm, where the air raid wardens also stored their equipment. One day I was in the dark entrance of the Blue House where I could see piles of grey blankets and materials for use by the air raid wardens. In front of me in a small room there were camp beds, mounds of grimy triangular bandages, splints and charts. I felt like Alice in Wonderland peering out from this tiny room at the green grass outside and the river flowing by.

Our leader was Miss Enid Colley, who had an office in North Parade. She had a loud voice, a stout figure and quickly made us realise that she was in charge. I was nervous of her at first but soon realised that she knew her first aid very thoroughly. I learnt the uses of triangular bandages and, when I went home, I bandaged my father's head, shoulders, legs and arms! We all laughed at the sight.

I was hooked and over the years I learnt to tie a reef knot, put on three different slings, recognise and attend to wounds and fractures, put on splints, resuscitate patients using Sylvester and Schaefer technique and to roller-bandage patients. At the end of each year, we took the general first aid examination and, on passing, could wear the grey dress, white frillies and head bandage with gloves tucked into the uniform. There were regular parades for all services; we used to assemble in Park Road, march along Christchurch Street West, down Bath Street to St John's Church for the service, for which we used to practise in the Blue House courtyard. I felt very proud because father was marching with the air raid wardens.

In 1944, I went to the Blue Anchor camp with all the Somerset cadets, where I learnt how to erect a bell tent. On Sundays we walked across the beach to Dunster for a church service, hurrying to catch the low tide; two cadets fainted during the service but they were well looked after! I returned to Blue Anchor in 1948 where we introduced French boys and girls to England after their ordeal during the war.

When I had passed further exams, I went to Victoria Hospital in Park Road to help to clean the wards. I spent a year teaching 5 year olds at Holy Trinity Primary School which was exhausting but a rewarding experience, which I put to good use at Fishponds College in Bristol. Several years later, I volunteered to care for the maternity patients in Yeovil Hospital.

Years afterwards, I realised how much had changed in the St John's Ambulance: no more hot sweet tea to treat shock, but much of the bandaging had remained the same.

Diana Crossman spoke eloquently of meeting Clara Grant at the unveiling of the plaque in November 2015. Her delightful memories of Willow Vale and Frome in the 1930s and 1940s were published in FSLS Yearbooks 17 and 18. Sadly, she died in February 2016. Ed

Rev WJE Bennett and the Silk Mill

On March 29, 1856 a special jury case was tried at the Somerset Spring Assizes in which Rev WJE Bennett was the plaintiff and the late Mr Henry Thompson defendant. The action was brought for the purpose of obtaining redress for an alleged grievance by reason of the smoke that came from the Silk Mill chimneys. At first Mr Bennett was nowhere. The opposing counsel, who was a schoolfellow at Westminster called Slade, exhibited the designs of the chimneys and appealed to Mr Bennett to point out the particular chimney that offended him. Mr Bennett confessed that he did not know which chimney, and the opposing counsel turned to the jury and said, 'Gentlemen, I am brought down all the way from London to defend this case, and the plaintiff does not know his own mind: does not know which chimney he objects to.' Mr Bennett, all this time, was the picture of despair, leaning hopelessly on his umbrella. The judge interfered at this point, exhorting Mr Bennett to try and collect his faculties and to say to which chimney he objected. In the silence of the court, Mr Bennett answered, 'My Lord, it is not the chimney at all that I object to; it is the smoke!'

The verdict was for Mr Bennett, damages forty shillings.

Extract from Somerset County Gazette 23.11.1878

A correspondence has taken place between Mr E Dickenson, of Berkeley House, Frome, and Col Everett of Greenhill, master of the South and West Wilts hounds to the following effect:

Berkeley House, February 11, 1878.

Berkeley House

My dear Sir, I understood you had fixed to go to Mells on Saturday, and postponed writing to you last week in consequence. I now write to say I think you had better not come there again. The place is full of foxes, there are no rabbits, and they have nothing to eat but pheasants. You are utterly unable to kill one, so I have directed my gamekeeper to try to poison them, and it is for this reason I write to you that a mishap may occur to your hounds. I have been over to Mells and have settled this this morning, as I see your programme for next week is arranged elsewhere, and I cannot wait, as I am losing pheasants, I believe daily.

Yours truly,
Edmund H Dickenson.

Greenhill, Warminster, February 13, 1878.

Dear Sir, I beg to acknowledge the receipt of your letter of the 11th Feb. I think on consideration you will agree with me that the tone is uncourteous. I beg to remark that the destruction of foxes by poison, at Mells would probably interfere with the national sport of fox hunting in all the district and in its neighbourhood, as foxes travel frequently between Batcombe, Postlebury and Mells; neither would hounds even follow their fox into Melcombe without fear of being poisoned. On consideration I should hardly think you could wish to destroy the sport of your other neighbours. As master of the South and West Wilts hounds, I am, in a certain degree acting as a servant of the public. I therefore feel it but right to send copies of your letter and, this, my reply, to the local press.

I am, Sir, yours faithfully,
John F Everett.

I am grateful to ALM for this correspondence. Ed

Obituary: Alan Yeates (9.X.1943-28.I.2016)

Alan was born in Midsomer Norton where his father owned the dairy; he had six older half siblings, but when his father died in 1945, there was no provision for him and he was brought up by his working mother and grandmother from London. They lived next to the Methodist chapel in High Street where Alan caught pneumonia that left him with lifelong chest problems. Alan passed the eleven plus but could not take up his place at Midsomer Norton Grammar School, however, after his apprenticeship as an electrician at the National Coal Board, he worked at Wells mental hospital and the RUH in Bath.

He changed careers, becoming a graphic designer with Abbey Engravers, making metal plates for printing pictures, a painstakingly detailed operation; this was a skill that he applied with great success in later life. Meanwhile Kate Jones, a teacher at Marshfield School, and Alan had met at a skittles match and they were married in 1978. When the printer in Bath closed, Alan and Kate did not wish to move with their children Robert and Megan; then, Alan worked in many capacities at Curry's being salesman, making deliveries and collecting debts until he retired in 2004, when they moved to Vernal Lane in Frome. Alan then took a two year on-line course in Computer Studies and was awarded his Diploma from Oxford University in 2006. It was at this time that Anne Wallis asked for help for collating and organising 'Contact'. He used his flair for design in producing many editions where his picture research proved invaluable. This was extended with the Yearbooks from 2011 onwards and the new editions of 'The Book of Frome' and 'A History of Mells' where he improved the illustrations, greatly enhancing the quality of both books as well as the design of 'The Butler and Tanner Story' and 'Willow Vale'. He also built the Frome Society website single handedly and kept it up to date over many years. Alan was a brilliant designer; he added style to FSLS publications in many of which his skill as a photographer played a key role. A further activity of which he was rightly proud, was the recording of Frome on Historypin with many hundreds of photographs of the town.

Alan was badly affected by the pneumonia he had suffered as a child; even so he had been a keen cyclist and ran a half marathon in Bath when he was over 50. In latter years, he suffered poor health and it was through his determination that he carried on, always striving to reach perfection in all that he did.

Alastair MacLeay